Isle of Dogs

Also by Clare Balding

My Animals and Other Family

Walking Home

Heroic Animals

The Racehorse Who Wouldn't Gallop

The Racehorse Who Disappeared

The Racehorse Who Learned to Dance

Fall Off, Get Back On, Keep Going

The Girl Who Thought She Was a Dog

Isle of Dogs

My canine adventure through Britain

CLARE BALDING

EBURY
PRESS

1

Ebury Press, an imprint of Ebury Publishing
20 Vauxhall Bridge Road
London SW1V 2SA

Ebury Press is part of the Penguin Random House group of companies
whose addresses can be found at global.penguinrandomhouse.com

First published by Ebury Press in 2023
www.penguin.co.uk

A CIP catalogue record for this book is available from the British Library

ISBN 9781529195392
Trade Paperback ISBN 9781529195408

Printed and bound in Great Britain by Clays Ltd, Elcograf S.p.A.

The authorised representative in the EEA is Penguin Random House
Ireland, Morrison Chambers, 32 Nassau Street, Dublin D02 YH68

Penguin Random House is committed to a sustainable future for
our business, our readers and our planet. This book is made
from Forest Stewardship Council® certified paper.

For Mum and Dad, who created a family full of dogs

Contents

Introduction

I was so lucky to grow up surrounded by dogs. The very first being I truly connected with as a kindred spirit was not my mother but her dog, Candy the boxer. Candy was the one I looked to for reassurance and support. She was the one who helped me transition from crawling to walking by allowing me to grab her rolls of excess skin and haul myself to my feet. She was the one who comforted me if I was crying. She was my playmate and, until my little brother was born, my one and only companion.

We had lurchers as well, but they were steadfastly aloof, interested more in the food I threw around than in me. As it happened, I threw around a lot of food, especially the mashed potato I didn't like from shepherd's pie, or bits of ham. I've never liked ham. Bertie and Cindy stayed close by my side whenever I was eating, as they never knew what might come their way. My mother says I am still unreasonably fussy. I would say I am selective, especially about tomatoes and pineapple.

Candy took her role as my protector very seriously, and I think she instilled in me a love for dogs that is part of my very soul. I spent most of my childhood thinking I was a dog. It seemed more fun than being a human.

I was once speaking at a children's literary festival in Jersey, when a little girl put up her hand to ask a question. She was only about four years old and had been considering my statement about thinking I was a dog.

'Can I ask, please, Clare Balding,' she said in a serious and thoughtful tone, 'when did you realise you weren't a dog?'

The audience laughed.

'And, Clare Balding, did you work it out for yourself or did your parents have to sit you down and tell you?'

I loved that image so much – my parents telling me to 'SIT' as they explained that I was not a dog – that I wrote a short book for World Book Day called *The Girl Who Thought She Was a Dog.* I have always hoped the little girl in Jersey who asked that question knows that she was its creative inspiration. I know plenty of children who have connected with the concept and plenty more who have taken to heart the motto of 'Be more dog!' In other words, prioritise the things that matter: love and friendship, playtime and exercise, sleep and food. If we put those things at the top of our list in life, we won't go far wrong.

As I grew into adulthood and work took off, however, the prospect of having a dog of my own started to look a little remote. I was travelling too much, there was no regularity to my schedule and I didn't have a house with a garden.

Then, in 2002, Alice and I got together. I say that as if it was an easy start to a relationship. It wasn't. I had to pass a stringent checklist of interests, habits and ambitions in life. No, I didn't want children; yes, I did want to travel; no, I didn't want to move out of London; yes, I would improve my golf (which was terrible); and yes, I would support her work. Alice finally agreed to live with me and said we could move anywhere in London, as long as it was Chiswick.

I had never really been to Chiswick, but it was on the right side of town for getting out to see my family so I agreed and we found a house with a garden that we could just about afford (with the help of a hefty mortgage). I only had one question:

'Can we get a dog?'

To me it was a commitment more important than asking someone to marry me. Not that we were allowed to do that in 2002, but still, the idea of finding someone with whom I could share a dog was my dream. Alice said yes.

So it was that Archie came into our lives, and was the key member of our family for fifteen and a half years. He came on staycations with us to smart hotels where he wasn't meant to sleep on the bed – yeah right, try telling that to a spoilt and wilful Tibetan terrier – and he occasionally accompanied me when I was recording *Ramblings* for Radio 4, although my producer Lucy wasn't that keen on him. This was mainly Archie's fault, because he had tried to bite her once.

Even though he's been gone now for nearly three years, I think about Archie every day, and not just because he's the screensaver on my phone. One day, I guess I'll change the photo, but it doesn't feel right just yet. He died during the lockdown summer of 2020, although he didn't just die in his sleep in the middle of the night. It hardly ever happens like that, does it?

We had to make the decision to have him put down. So it's our fault. We played God. It's a horrible choice to make and anyone who has ever been in the same situation will understand that, when you know, you know. My mother had always told me it was better to go a week too soon than a week too late; you can't put a dog through pain and discomfort with no hope of recovery. It's just not fair. So we made the fateful call.

It happened during very tight Covid restrictions, so we couldn't go into the vet's surgery to be with him, but maybe that was for the best. I would have cried uncontrollably and that would have upset him. Instead, we entrusted him into the arms of his favourite vet, Vesi, and she gently took him away from us.

He always loved the vet's surgery. I think it's because he knew he would get a treat and he was a very greedy dog, so he wagged his tail as she lifted him up and he looked very happy to be going inside. He didn't know, of course, that he would never be coming home again.

Archie had lived a full and active life. We knew the end was coming when he didn't want to go for a walk any more and his back end had lost its stability. He was not a perfect dog, but God, I miss him.

Introduction

I miss everything a dog brings to daily life – the walks on a frosty morning, the gatherings in the park with fellow dog owners for a 10am coffee, the enthusiastic greeting when I got back from working away, the cuddles (when he felt like it) on the sofa.

Yes, I know we had to warn the kids not to go near him if he was on the back of the sofa because he may suddenly launch an attack. Yes, I know he hated the black Labrador who lived over the road, and he might growl at any larger dog in a manner that was downright unfriendly and plain stupid, given that he was half their size. Yes, I know that if he had a pair of socks that he wanted to 'hide' or a chew that he had decided to bury in the garden, it was not a good idea to try and take them away from him. I now know this is called a 'guarding instinct' and we had to distract him to avoid confrontation. As I said, he wasn't perfect, but I still miss him.

Archie was a black and white Tibetan terrier. His grandfather, the comically named Fabulous Willy, won Best in Show at Crufts in 2007. I was presenting the programme when he became champion and so naturally I knew his owners and his breeder, Ken Sinclair. Knowing how much it would mean to them all, my hand was shaking as I held the microphone and attempted to interview them after their moment of victory. We were all close to tears. The ultimate prize in the dog-showing world had been won, for the first time, by a Tibetan terrier.

The coolest customer in the main arena at the Birmingham NEC was Willy himself. He sat there on the table, long hair flowing like fine, glossy silk, posing serenely for the cameras. He was totally untroubled by the fuss around him.

His grandson Archie was never destined for the show ring. We thought he was handsome and perfect in every way, but the breeder always knows which pups have that show-ring X factor and tend to hang on to them.

When we visited Araki kennels in Gloucestershire to pick a puppy, we had to answer all sorts of questions and fill out a form with details of where we lived, whether we had a garden, whether we knew how to care for a dog. If any breeder doesn't do this, by the way, you should be wary. The best of them are rigorous in their interrogation of new owners.

Archie dominated his litter, climbing all over them to come and say hello to us. He kissed me as I held him and sucked my chin, which of course I thought was a sign that he had picked us. His confidence probably should have been a warning of the issues we would later have with his dominance. He thought he was top dog. During the research for this book I have learned a lot about how this can lead to insecurity in a dog, as they always think they have to protect their patch. No wonder he was so angry with the Labrador who lived over the road for daring to invade 'his space'.

Archie's passion worked both ways. When he hated someone, he was all in, but when he loved he was equally committed. He had a bit of a thing for whippets and so when he met Sid, he fell head over heels. Sid's owners, Chris and Derek, have been firm friends of ours ever since

– they had to be, given Archie's determination to make Sid love him.

Equally, Dougal the cairn terrier, who cared little for Archie's affection, brought Joss and David into our lives. Maggie and Richard owned a gentle giant of a Great Dane called Jess, and Dariel owned a Tibetan terrier called Sunny who was rather more zen than Archie and never snapped at anyone.

Our gang of dogs gathered almost daily and therefore so did we. A group of folks of different ages, backgrounds, careers, life experiences and interests – all united by our dogs.

It's a story that is repeated across the nation. Friends made through dogs creating a bond that lasts far beyond the lifespan of our canine family. Sid, Dougal, Sunny, Jess and Archie have all gone now, but the bond between us humans remains. I have met so many people whose daily walks with their group of dog friends have been their mainstay, have got them through grief, stress at work or at home, helped them deal with loneliness and built their confidence. It's medicine for the soul.

I am fascinated by the impact dogs have on our lives, the characteristics they display themselves and bring out in us and even how they influence our choice of friends, how we live, where we go on holiday and the sort of jobs that we want to do. *Isle of Dogs* is an exploration of the way dogs have shaped and influenced the people of the United Kingdom.

It is a telling of our national story not through the usual metrics of wars, monarchy or politics, but through our dogs.

* * *

Why are we drawn to certain breeds and what does that say about us? What has changed in the way we look after our dogs, and how has their role in society altered through the centuries? We have certainly moved away from keeping dogs outside in kennels and far more of us have them in our homes, on our sofas and (hands up as guilty on this one) sleeping on our beds at night.

My parents, until recently, had an ageing lurcher called Mac and a boxer called Boris. The latter is as badly behaved as his name might suggest, with no heed of recall and no understanding of personal space – which, given his size (he is a beast), is an issue when he enthusiastically greets young children, elderly people or anyone with balance issues.

The sofas and chairs in their sitting room are covered in books – not because my parents love to read, but in an attempt to persuade the dogs not to climb on the furniture. Consequently, any human who wants to sit on a sofa has to rearrange a library of books. I've suggested a removable cover would be more attractive. Or, of course, training, but it's too late for that.

Boris has been known to sit up on a chair at the kitchen table expecting full service, and whenever the dishwasher is being stacked, he likes to add a personal prewash to the plates. Even my mother might concede that Boris is the worst-behaved dog she has ever had, but on the plus side, he is very affectionate and funny.

Sadly, Mac reached the end of his glorious run in the spring of 2023. He lived longer than any lurcher our family had ever had. He always got up to greet visitors with his tail wagging and a grin on his face. In those last weeks he became less mobile and gradually less responsive, not wanting to eat or go for a walk. The decision was inevitable but painful and it doesn't matter how old you are when you lose a dog, you cry like a child.

Mac has left a huge hole in my parents' lives and we expected poor Boris to be bereft. In truth, he seems to have got over it rather quickly. It has meant an unchallenged position at the dishwasher to 'help' with the plates and if he sits next to my father at the dining room table, he can be guaranteed a good tasting menu. He is too old now to reform and, like my father, his behaviour is only going one way – and that's not towards improvement.

* * *

Those who invest the time and commitment into training dogs have reaped the benefits of their extraordinary gifts. They can help people in all sorts of ways; we have made use of their superior senses to root out drugs, discover disease, detect bombs, rescue missing or injured people and sniff out accelerants in potential cases of arson. Dogs are amazing.

Archie was not particularly gifted or well trained, but he seemed well suited to us. The reason Alice and I picked a Tibetan terrier was fairly straightforward. They don't shed hair, which was essential as Alice is allergic to animal hair. A Tibetan terrier is small enough to pick up but strong enough to go on long walks, which was perfect for me. They are intelligent, loyal and full of character. They are good guard dogs but don't yap without cause.

Tibetan terriers have been around for about 2,000 years. Originating in the Lost Valley of Tibet, they were considered bringers of good luck and were treated as members of the family, referred to as 'the little people'. They could act as a babysitter, sheep or goat herder, guard dog or companion. Their shaggy double coat protected them against high winds and the cold of winter while in the summer their coats would be shaved off and woven into cloth. The dogs had to survive at altitude in very thin air and were renowned for their endurance.

I always believed that Archie had hidden powers of perception and that he could judge people from a distance. Maybe it's true – he certainly picked good friends for us. He was not that keen to learn tricks, unless there were treats on offer, in which case he was more than eager to please.

* * *

I know it is the given British convention that you have to be either a dog OR a cat person. You cannot possibly be both. I wonder if it's a version of snobbery to look down on cat people; the stereotype of the 'mad cat lady' doesn't help. As someone who did not grow up with cats, I have been guilty in the past of falling into the trap of thinking dogs (and by extension, dog owners) are vastly superior.

Well, I'd better do the equivalent of going through the red channel at the airport and admit I have something to declare: we now have two cats. They are mother and son British shorthairs called Button and Eric. They are very sweet and beautiful but I would never suggest that they either obey commands or give two hoots about how Alice or I feel. They give us attention if they fancy a treat and Eric is particularly adept at standing by the fridge and giving me doe eyes and a little bit of affection until he gets more fish. He has been known to actually jump into the fridge to point at the fish. Now I think that's quite clever.

Button likes it when I'm in the study. She climbs on the desk and walks all over the keyboard until I open the drawer and give her a disgusting smelly biscuit thing.

Cats are too independent and too cool to give in to sentimental simpering. Having said that, whenever we come back from holiday they make a point of sleeping on the bed for at least the first two nights. Button will often kiss Alice's nose to wake her up, and she kids herself that it's driven by love rather than hunger. When Button moves on to flexing her toenails on Alice's head, it's not as loving.

I have a very posh aunt who has said to me disparagingly, 'I can't believe you have cats,' as if it is a crime against society. She stopped herself from saying 'so common', but I know that's what she was thinking.

For the sake of my aunt, my mother and all those who will find it hard to forgive me for allowing cats to come into this book at all, that is where I will leave any talk about Button and Eric, except to reiterate that you can like dogs AND cats.

Anyway, this is a book about dogs and the cats won't give a damn about that, because that's the way they are.

* * *

In the course of my research I will travel across Britain meeting a variety of owners, breeders and dog experts, finding out as much as I can about our canine companions. I will meet dogs who do everything for their owners: from waking them up in the morning to unloading the washing machine. I will find out how people care for and train dogs that are as large as a pony or small enough to fit in a handbag. I will discover why certain breeds have soared in popularity, and why it was that our relationship with dogs changed during Queen Victoria's reign. There are a vast number of businesses that thrive because of our love of dogs, so I will visit doggy day care centres and talk to professional dog walkers and a dog listener.

The other, more personal quest is for us to find another dog to make our little family complete. I do not intend to rush that decision, but if it comes as a by-product of visiting so many doggy people and places, then I would consider it serendipity. My father has always maintained that when a dog dies you cannot replace that individual but you can fill the space they leave. Anyone who has ever loved and lost a dog will appreciate the huge hole in the empty kitchen every morning when you go to make breakfast for a dog that is no longer there.

We are famed as a nation of dog lovers, but I wonder whether any of us truly appreciate how much our lives, and our history, have been shaped by our connection to canines. This is an adventure, an exploration and a voyage of discovery across our Isle of Dogs.

CHAPTER 1

Dogs Becoming Pets

I've just come in from a walk. It still feels odd to be doing so without a lead in my hand and a dog running beside me, but I smile at everyone else's dogs and namecheck the breeds as I pass them. Today a miniature schnauzer, an Irish terrier, two lovely golden retrievers with tummies blackened by mud, a couple of Labradors and a few cockapoos smiled back at me. I like to test myself by naming dog breeds so will constantly check whether I'm right.

'Is that a lagotto romagnolo?' I'll say to the owner of a gorgeous milk-chocolate and cream curly-coated dog who bounds up to say hello. I'm thrilled when he says yes and points out that most people think it's a labradoodle. I smile with a hint of self-congratulation. It's pathetic, I know, but I'm competitive even with myself.

The most enthusiastic and adorable lagotto romagnolo won Crufts in 2023, so more people are now aware of the breed. She was a four-year-old bitch called Orca and she had travelled with her handler, Javier, and owner Ante from Croatia. What I liked about her most was that she didn't require edible treats to put on a show; she had a squeaky toy which Javier held as she stood perfectly square, wagging her tail. She enjoyed her day in the spotlight and shone for the judge who I think was impressed as much by her personality as her conformation and condition. It all matters, and the perfect package is rewarded with glory.

One of the perks of having presented Crufts for nearly two decades on the TV, both for the BBC and for Channel 4, is that I have seen every different breed of dog and I make it my mission to remember as many as I can. In 2023 there were 222 different breeds across the seven groups. Crufts is a massive show, the biggest dog show in the world, with a dedicated area called Discover Dogs, where you can meet and learn about the characteristics and history of all of the breeds.

Did you know that at the start of the 19th century there were fewer than 20 known breeds across the UK? By the dawning of the 20th century that had tripled, but it was in the next hundred years that the sub-sections really multiplied, and it is estimated that across the world there may be as many as 400 different breeds of dog.

At Crufts you can learn about all of them, and you can also see dogs at work, showcasing the traits unique to their breeds: doing agility, in flyball races, obedience classes and demonstrations. Those demos range from police dogs showing off their skills at bringing down a criminal to a group of kind and willing golden retrievers performing a group line dance. There is nearly always one dog who either doesn't feel like it or gets confused, and it always makes me laugh when the others stay glued to their owners' ankles while one dog sits in the middle looking at the crowd.

A dog must win its age group, its gender and then go head to head – so it's always best bitch against best dog for Best of Breed. Those breed winners then go into the group judging. The breeds are divided across seven different groups: Terriers, breeds well suited to catch small pests like rats and mice. The name derives from old French *chien terrier* and Latin *terra* – meaning dog of the earth. Hounds, independent hunting dogs that are either sight hounds like greyhounds and whippets or scent hounds like beagles and bloodhounds. Gundogs like retrievers, spaniels and pointers, which traditionally assisted hunters in the field. They are renowned for their patience and willingness to please. Working dogs, breeds that make good guard and police dogs, like dobermans and rottweilers, or freight haulers like malamutes and huskies. Pastoral dogs, which are often used for herding and protecting livestock – breeds such as Old English sheepdogs and border collies. Toy dogs, which tend to be smaller and were considered lap warmers or companion dogs, such as pugs and Chihuahuas. Finally, there are utility dogs, a broad category that covers everything else. It includes Dalmatians, French bulldogs and shih-tzus. Most groups feature about 30 breeds and the winner of each group will go forward to Best in Show.

The popularity of a dog breed always spikes after they win Crufts – largely because their photo is on the front page of every newspaper and leading the news bulletins. When I first worked on the coverage in 2005, Best in Show was won by a very bonny little Norfolk terrier called Coco. They are the smallest of the terrier breeds and the way I remember the difference between Norfolk and Norwich terriers is that the Norwich has sticking-up ears like a witch's hat, whereas the Norfolk has droopy ears, like a – well, like a hat with ear flaps. They are the colour of a Hobnob biscuit with a small tail that curls over the back.

A Norfolk terrier stands at about ten inches tall and has a coat that is wiry and straight on top, soft underneath. They need to be brushed regularly with hand stripping in the autumn and the spring. They are active, intelligent and have bags of character. Plus (and this really is a bonus) they love humans. In the case of the Norfolk terrier, I can absolutely understand the appeal.

Every Christmas I do a whistle-stop tour of my London-based godchildren to drop off presents and catch up on their news. Alice came with me last year (because it was raining and the golf course was shut) and when we arrived at my godson George's house we were greeted by their adorable Norfolk terrier, Toast. She gave one small bark and then wagged her tail. Minutes later she was curled up on Alice's lap on the sofa, fast asleep.

'I think we'd better get going,' I said after half an hour, as we were due at the next godchild's house. It's all very quick and efficient, you see. I know that my questions and a teen-ager's answers are fairly limited. Leave them wanting more, or at least not wanting less.

'I can't move,' Alice said, looking down at Toast.

She was properly smitten and, despite her allergies, didn't even cough, which gives me hope that our potential new dog could come from a wider selection than I'd initially thought. Norfolk terriers have therefore unsurprisingly worked their way on to my shortlist of PND (Potential Next Dog).

Back to my dog-less walk. It's a really pretty route through the park, down to the river, watching the rowers in the freezing cold battling with the current, making the most of the pale winter light silhouetting the leafless trees, seeing house lights start to turn on in the late afternoon before heading back down a path through the woods in the park. It was one of Archie's favourite routes when he was younger, before he got old and stiff and tired. At least I think it was one of his favourites – how do we know when they can't talk to us?

I believe we know because they reflect our mood. They wag their tails and we smile so they wag their tails even more. Dogs can sense when we're happy and that makes them happy. It's a simple equation and it's part of why our rela-tionship has developed from hunting companions and guard dogs into companion animals that are part of the family. They can also sense when we're sad and offer comfort and support. It may well be that this response is based on their supreme sense of smell. If we are stressed or under pressure, we emit a different odour. They can smell that something is wrong and they respond accordingly.

Dogs have far more empathy than any other animal I've come across. Horses are kind and noble but they don't live our everyday lives with us. Donkeys are steadfast and loyal but devoted to each other rather than us. Parrots are clever and I hear can be consoling but I've never been great with flying beasts. I think it's because a bat got into my bedroom when I was very young and terrorised me.

My friend and brilliant Crufts commentator Jessica Holm (who has drawn the illustrations for this book) had an African grey parrot called Oscar, who used to impersonate the sounds around the house like the washing machine or the microwave. He could also whistle for the dogs, which left them confused. Oscar was wicked and ingenious. She now has Nigel, a blue-fronted Amazon parrot who can perfectly perform the theme tunes to *Harry Potter*, *Game of Thrones* and *The Addams Family*. He occasionally throws in a bit of opera for variety.

Not as good at mimicry, but far more cuddly, are Jessica's French bulldogs who, she says, 'have no understanding of personal space at all'. They surround her on the sofa and if a stranger comes into the house, once the cacophony of barking has subsided, they will quickly try to sit on their face. They love unconditionally and cannot conceive of ever not being happy with life.

French bulldogs have become one of the most popular breeds in the UK and regularly appear at the top of the charts alongside Labradors. They were developed in the mid-19th century from toy bulldogs (who themselves were the smallest of the British bulldogs bred with each other to create a lighter, shorter, altogether miniature version) that had been taken to France by lacemakers relocating from Nottingham to Normandy.

Their quirk is that they have 'bat ears' which stand up, giving them an even more comical look. Funnily enough, the original exporters of toy bulldogs to France sent the ones with sticking-up ears because they thought them inferior. The quirky ears were embraced by the French and, in 1906, the Kennel Club officially recognised the *bouledogue Français* (the name changed to French bulldog in 1912) as a separate breed.

They have been made even more popular around the world by celebrity owners like Lady Gaga, Madonna, Leonardo DiCaprio and Dwayne 'The Rock' Johnson. They are undeniably cute but also come with a major health warning of breathing issues if their faces are too flat. If you want a Frenchie, make sure you go to a reputable breeder who is consciously trying to develop the breed according to the new Kennel Club standards that promote longer noses. Otherwise you will be left with a litany of problems, large bills from the vet and a dog who cannot breathe well enough to take enough exercise. I don't want to be a doom-monger, but if I can achive one thing with this book, it will be to make us all think hard about where we are sourcing our dogs and to take more responsibility for doing due diligence on the breed and its background.

Labradors – or Labrador retrievers to give them their official name – are the perennial favourites in British homes. My sister-in-law Anna Lisa had a very obedient and loyal Labrador called Puddle. Anna Lisa is one of those women who really can do it all. She is tall, beautiful and elegant, she can organise an army of teenage children, run a business, deal with complicated travel logistics, cope with hundreds of owners descending on the stables for breakfast, solve disputes, staffing crises and, on top of all that, she cooks to gourmet chef level. She can also train her dogs to actually listen to and obey commands. Most women would feel intimidated but Alice and I are just grateful she's on our team in life. It's like having Wonder Woman (the Gal Gadot version) as a mate.

When she first met my brother, Anna Lisa owned Puddle, while my brother had a mad and disobedient boxer called Tonto. I know, there is a recurring theme in our family of badly behaved boxers. I blame the parents.

The discipline of Puddle never really wore off on Tonto and the same could be said of the humans, but the yin and yang seems to work. More than two decades later, they are still happily married with three children – and two boxers who are scrupulously well-trained (by Anna Lisa).

My grandmother also always had a Lab, although the one I knew best – Chico – was so ruled by his stomach that he would regularly open the fridge and help himself to a shoulder of ham or a lamb chop. She ended up having to put a bicycle padlock around the door handles.

The British love a Labrador, and this was illustrated during lockdown when two Labradors called Olive and Mabel became internet sensations. My friends Andrew Cotter and Caroline Short are their proud parents and I'm in Cheshire to meet them.

Caroline used to work with me as a producer at Radio 5 Live and Andrew is a commentator across a range of sports including rugby union, athletics, golf, tennis and the Boat Race. His voice has been listened to by millions of sports fans, but no one, least of all him, could have predicted the reaction when he put his commentary to the daily action of his dogs. He described with gravitas the two of them eating their breakfast, jumping in a lake, playing with their toys or going to the beach. The public loved their adventures, viewing the videos more than 100 million times.

Olive is the elder and supposedly wiser of the two, while Mabel follows along with a confused look on her face into whatever trouble might be occurring. Olive is black and Mabel is yellow.

'All Labradors are cheery souls – they are life's great optimists,' Andrew told me, perhaps failing to recognise that his own negative outlook on life requires the balance of his dogs. 'Olive is slightly more distant, where Mabel is more affectionate and tactile. She clambers all over you on the sofa, whereas if you go in for a cuddle with Olive, she will not be amused.'

Olive and Mabel have fans as far afield as America and Australia, including the actor Ryan Reynolds and the wonderful writer, comedian, actress and all-round good egg Dawn French. They have their own dedicated YouTube channel and receive fan mail from millions of people whose lockdown was cheered up by their antics.

In March 2020, the world of sport came to a standstill and therefore Andrew's work stopped. The weekend that he was meant to commentate on the Boat Race, he posted the first video of Olive and Mabel racing each other to finish their breakfast.

He was amazed by the feedback. In the world of social media, where so much can be critical or negative, almost every comment he received on Twitter or Instagram was positive and supportive. The fans demanded more and so suddenly Andrew was required to come up with further ideas, commentary and films. A book was commissioned, a newspaper column began and they have even been on tour.

Olive and Mabel are blissfully unaware of their fame, although they clearly enjoy the attention of an audience. I helped out on stage at Richmond Theatre in London when Andrew took the Olive and Mabel show on the road. During the second half, he let the dogs loose in the audience. Caroline was hovering in the wings in case she needed to round them up, but the two of them roamed the aisles saying hello to everyone and grabbing a treat if it was offered. I'm not sure many people would trust their dogs in that scenario, but they are, as Andrew tells them every day, very good dogs.

I am particularly fond of Mabel, mainly because she is routinely referred to as being less savvy than Olive. She is always pleased to see me – in fairness, she is always pleased to see anyone – and I feel she needs sticking up for in a house that clearly tells Olive how clever she is ALL THE TIME.

I pretend that I go to stay with Andrew and Caroline because it's handy when I'm in Salford for work. It's not that handy at all, but I like seeing the dogs and catching up with all their news. When Caroline and I take them for a walk in the local woods, people say, 'Gosh, those dogs look just like Olive and Mabel from the internet.'

'I know,' replies Caroline before she calls them by name. 'Remarkably similar.'

The other walkers always look confused, unsure whether she is winding them up or telling the truth. It's a bit like when people say to me, 'You look just like Clare Balding.'

'Really?' I say.

'So much like her but not as …'

I wait for the inevitable.

'Not as big.'

Well, that's always charming. I'll make sure to pass that on when I see her.

More fun is when someone shouts 'Sue, Sue, give us a wave' and I have to stop myself swearing at them or giving them an offensive gesture just for the fun of making them think that Sue Barker is rude. She's not, by the way. Just in case you were in any doubt.

Lovely as Labradors are, though, I always worry that owning them is a bit unoriginal. Like wearing a Schöffel gilet at Badminton Horse Trials, there is a danger of fitting in with the crowd to such an extent that blending becomes bland. Case in point: on their way back from a holiday with dog-loving friends in Wales, Anna Lisa called her Labrador Henry (the successor to Puddle) to get into the boot of the car. The dog duly obliged and off they went. As they got onto the M4, the phone rang. It was their friend saying, 'I think you've got our dog.'

They had to turn back to complete the swap.

I mean, I don't want to be too rude, but if you can't tell which one is your dog, what's the point?

Having said all of that, Alice and I will soon be visiting a charity called Dogs for Good, where they train dogs to do all sorts of assistance jobs. All of their puppies are Labrador/ golden retriever-crosses because they respond so well to training. Part of the key to that is being 'food driven'. It's the stomach ruling their brains again – if a treat is on offer, they will do anything.

Empathy is why dogs rather than cats (with the odd exception) are the ones who go into hospitals or care homes and can provide assistance to human beings in need. Their obedience and willingness to please is why they can be trained to detect disease, bombs or drugs. At the risk of anthropomorphism, I would suggest that loyalty is why they bond to us as individuals.

We need dogs as much as they need us, and never was that more obvious than during the first Covid outbreak when lockdown forced so many of us to work from home. Dog ownership expanded exponentially during that time, and for most people it transformed their life and family relationships.

One third of British households now has at least one dog. There are around 13 million dogs across our islands. That's a figure that has risen markedly since 2011, when data suggested a dog population of around 7.6 million. Dog-owning households jumped in that time from 23 per cent to 34 per cent.

I spoke to Professor Philip Howell of Cambridge University, author of *At Home and Astray: The Domestic Dog in Victorian Britain*, about when the change happened from dogs being kept outside in kennels and being regarded as working partners to dogs coming inside to be part of the family. There is evidence of dogs being kept in the home before the Victorian era, particularly in large country houses where the aristocracy favoured the combination of sporting dogs and small companion dogs, or in the homes of labourers and farm workers who were more likely to keep terriers and herding dogs, but Howell is specific about a mass adoption of the concept of dogs as pets.

'The normalisation of the idea of the pet being an animal kept in the house primarily for companionship happens in the 1860s,' he tells me. 'I would even call it the "age of the pet" when society as a whole tends to accept that pet-keeping is normal-ish, natural-ish and largely desirable. It becomes more acceptable for people of quality, for middle-class people, to have dogs in their own homes.'

Howell adds: 'When you look at the rest of the world, we are the outliers. Having a dog in the house is an oddity. Other countries and cultures have dogs roaming around but not inside the house. They are in the yard or on the streets and that's perfectly normal.'

I remember being at the Olympics in Athens in 2004 and coming across very clean and healthy-looking dogs who lived outside on the streets. We would have classed them as 'strays' but they seemed to have their own zone and were perfectly content to roam within it. As it turned out, the local government had rounded up every dog to neuter them, jab them with various vaccinations and give them all a good bath and a brush. They didn't try and force them into kennels or put them down, they just cleaned them up and put them back in what they saw as their 'natural' environment.

We need to understand that different dogs need different lifestyles and that we can't impose our ideas without recognising that we don't always get it right. As Professor Howell says, maybe it's us Brits who are the odd ones out, but I'm happy to be part of our nation of dog lovers and am impatient to welcome another dog into our lives.

As Alice and I start our search, we need to think about what sort of life we will be able to give our new family member. We don't live on a farm, so a border collie or any of the hyper-energetic breeds that need endless exercise would not be a sensible option. A terrier would be lovely, although I appreciate they can have their own ideas about what they want to do and where they want to go. I am very keen on the intelligence and general demeanour of poodles and I have also been won over by the charm of the miniature schnauzer. We don't have children so we can cope easily with a dog that needs its own space and we will make sure it has plenty of exercise without overdoing it. We can offer love and safety in a calm environment but with plenty of opportunity for playtime with other dogs. I feel as if I am writing a CV for a job and, in a way, I guess I am. We need to examine ourselves and our lifestyle, make changes if needed and improve as best we can so that we are worthy of a dog.

CHAPTER 2

The Kennel Club, London

The key to every job I do is research. I have even been fond of saying 'facts are my friend', which makes me sound like a person with no friends at all. I do have friends. Honestly I do. However, I like a bit of digging into the history books, whether that be about women's football in the early 20th century, the origination of skeleton (as in the winter sport, which seems to have started with drunken British men in St Moritz sliding down the icy roads for a laugh), or the history of our different dog breeds. I enjoy the homework and it gives me stuff to say in the event of having to fill. That's TV talk for when things don't work out, or when it suddenly rains and the presenter has to keep waffling on for however long it takes for the next film to be ready or the interviewee to arrive. It's my favourite part of the job when things go tits up: that's when I really earn my money. So, I begin this job as I do any other, with research. Today, I am visiting the Kennel Club central offices in London, which house a vast amount of information.

There is no better place to start my investigation into the dogs of our history.

The Kennel Club was founded in 1873 by a Conservative MP called Sewallis Shirley, along with 12 other men. Their aim was to ensure fairness and consistency across the growing number of dog shows and field trials, as well as to protect and regulate the different pedigree breeds. The first dog show on record was held in 1859 in Newcastle, where entries were restricted to setters and pointers. Later that year in Birmingham, non-sporting breeds were allowed to compete. In 1860 the Birmingham Dog Show had 267 entries from 30 different breeds. By the end of that decade, the National Dog Show was drawing in more than 700 dogs and selling over 20,000 tickets to interested spectators.

London soon got in on the act, with 100,000 people coming to a week-long event in Chelsea in 1863. The Kennel Club organised and hosted big shows at Crystal Palace in south London and Alexandra Palace in north London.

By the time dog-biscuit salesman Charles Cruft started his eponymous all-breed show in 1891, there were hundreds of dog shows, large and small, up and down the country. In 1863 the first dog show in Paris took place and from 1877, the Westminster Kennel Club Dog Show set a similar trend in America, but it really all began in Britain.

Membership of the Kennel Club remained male-only until 1979. The woman who changed things was Florence Nagle, and suffice to say there's a whole book to be written about her. I originally knew of her because of her role in transforming horse racing. She was the one who got the rules changed so that women could hold a training licence.

When 20 years of persuasion, logic and reason didn't work on the Jockey Club, she sued them. She had been training her horses for decades, but under the arcane and misogynistic rules, her Head Lad was the official holder of the licence. Mrs Nagle successfully argued her case with the backing of three judges who described the Jockey Club's stance as 'restrictive and nonsensical' and 'arbitrary and capricious'. She was granted a training licence in her own name in the summer of 1966. The ruling came just too late for my maternal grandmother to have taken over the training licence when her husband died and the beneficiary was my father, who had recently arrived as assistant trainer.

As well as being a good judge of horses, Florence Nagle was an outstanding breeder of dogs. She didn't go small. Irish wolfhounds were her thing, and she was the first person to start exporting her stock across Europe and to America. She had countless national champions but achieved the ultimate prize when Sulhamstead Merman, an Irish wolfhound she had bred, owned and handled, won Best in Show at Cruft's in 1960.

She was a highly respected judge of various hound breeds and a keen competitor in field trials with Irish setters, and yet for all this expertise and commitment, she was not allowed to be a member of the Kennel Club. She could be

chair of the Ladies Committee – a sub-set with no responsibility or decision-making powers – but she was denied
membership of the club itself, so at the age of 83 she went to
court once again, on behalf of all women.

The case was dismissed on a legal technicality, but before
she could launch an appeal, the Kennel Club chairman saw
sense and changed the constitution to admit female members.

I am sure I met Florence Nagle once at Kempton Park,
where she sponsored a race for female apprentice jockeys. She
would have been in her 90s by then and I was an ignorant
teenager with big ideas about equality and not a clue that I
was standing next to a feminist pioneer. I wish I had taken the
opportunity to talk to her properly.

'This was a matter of principle,' she once said of her
battle against the patriarchal governing bodies. 'I am a feminist and I believe in equal rights for women. Things should be
decided by ability, not sex.'

Yup, Florence, you're spot on. I wish you were still
around, because there are just a few things I wouldn't mind
getting your help on …

When she died in 1988, she left money for the apprentice
race to continue as she believed it was important to encourage
girls to come into racing and, probably even more important,
to motivate owners and trainers to give them opportunities.
She'd be pleased to see the progress that has been made and
the huge success of Rachael Blackmore over jumps and Hollie
Doyle on the flat.

In the dog world, female breeders, owners and exhibitors make up over half of the entrants to Crufts. Vast numbers of women help run the show, most of the volunteers at rescue centres are women and there are more female vets (and certainly more female veterinary nurses) than male. There is yet to be a female chair of the Kennel Club but I am sure that is just a matter of time. Things move slowly at organisations like the Kennel Club and the Jockey Club.

Speaking of time, the Kennel Club is celebrating a landmark anniversary and has been granted a Royal prefix in honour of the occasion. The entrance is adorned with flags with 150 YEARS emblazoned upon them. I am hoping they will help with navigation, because Alice has been recording her show for Mellow Magic Radio just off Piccadilly and has agreed, somewhat reluctantly, to come and meet me in Clarges Street. It's not that she didn't want to, it's just that she didn't see the point.

'You're only half a mile up the road,' I say. 'It will take literally ten minutes to walk here.'

'Don't use "literally". It's lazy. And it's inaccurate.' She does a good impression of my favourite English teacher at school. 'And I don't walk as fast as you. Also there are people to dodge and it might be raining.'

I smile and mentally wag my tail like a Labrador pleading for food. I tell her it would be really helpful because she might ask questions I wouldn't think of. The intellectual argument works and – despite the Himalayan challenges of

41

walking in a straight line on a pavement in London – she is on her way.

* * *

Ciara Farrell has worked at the Kennel Club library for 17 years, and it's safe to say that there is no one (possibly in the world) who knows more about canine literature. She has a degree in English and history, a Master's in librarianship and information studies and she is currently doing another Master's in public history. Her knowledge of dogs, and books about dogs, has been learned on the job, and my word, she has absorbed an ocean full of knowledge.

The Kennel Club library is free to enter for members of the public and as I emerge from the lift I hear the barking of Bob, a friendly Portuguese water dog who announces the arrival of every individual. He comes out to say hello and leans against my legs. He has short-cut black hair with flecks of grey. Portuguese water dogs are strong swimmers who were bred to help fishermen either by retrieving nets or even herding fish towards the nets. They also love people, which is always a handy quality, and they don't shed hair so they're hypoallergenic. President Obama and his family had two Portuguese water dogs called Bo and Sunny.

I have come back to the library to do some research, although if I'm being honest I am really here to download Ciara's brain.

The first thing Ciara is showing me is the oldest book in the Kennel Club's collection. It's called *De Canibus Britannicis* and it was published in 1570.

It's in a cardboard box, wrapped in tissue paper and is no bigger than my hand. The cover is brown leather and the edges of the pages have coloured as if they've been dipped in coffee. It's in remarkably good condition for a book that dates back nearly 500 years.

The author, Johannes Caius (as in Gonville and Caius College, Cambridge) describes various dog types and separates them into groups according to their purpose or function.

In his everyday life, Dr John Caius was the personal physician to Edward VI, Queen Mary and Elizabeth I. Ciara turns the pages and I see that it's written in Latin. I studied Latin for A level but I'm not about to reveal that because she might ask me to translate and I am self-aware enough to be sure that I will only embarrass myself with my lack of ability.

This detailed account of dogs is an interesting diversion for a man who was elected nine times as the president of the College of Physicians.

'What we're looking at are the dogs Dr John Caius saw around him in Elizabethan England,' Ciara says. 'There are no made-up dogs, no magical dogs, just the dogs he observed working and living in the country at the time. This is a first edition and it is likely that it's the copy he gave to the College of Medicine.

'I love it,' she continues, because he's got such a vivid voice and the dogs seem relatable. There are earlier descriptions of dogs in medieval times where you can read about hunting dogs, but this book is the most comprehensive one that gives you an insight into all sorts of working dogs.'

The dogs are split into groups, not unlike the Working, Pastoral and Gundog groups I know from Crufts. There's also the beginning of an idea of Toy dogs like the Queen's 'comforter spaniel' that are deliberately bred to be small enough to sit on the lap and act as a companion.

Ciara tells me about a breed that no longer exists called the 'turn-spit dog'. Poor little thing was like a hamster in a wheel, running round and round to turn a spit over a fire.

'They're famously not happy doing their work,' Ciara says.

I'm not surprised. It sounds like an awful life.

'They're mentioned in memoirs and letters and they're always trying to run away. They weren't treated very well.'

Ciara is a historian, so she's more emotionally robust than me. I am virtually in tears over a dog I had never heard of before and a breed that died out at the end of the 18th century because technology removed the need for its dreadful purpose in life. I'm quite glad that staring at the Latin words doesn't make it any clearer as to what the dog was like. Ciara tells me that their job became obsolete and they didn't quite make it into the modern period of dogs as leisure and companion animals, dogs in showing or breeding as a hobby.

If they'd hung on another 30 years we might still have them, but we don't.

So that was that for the turn-spit dog. We'd barely know about them if it wasn't for this text. This first edition of *De Canibus Britannicis* has no illustrations so I can only imagine what they looked like. Even Ciara admits that, written in Latin and with no drawings, the book is 'probably a little bit dry'.

'But it was translated into English only seven years later!' she says, and with another flourish she produces a sheaf of pages in a folder with protective plastic sleeves.

'This is a 1606 English copy that I've got here and it's incorporated into a bigger encyclopaedia called *The History of Four-footed Beasts*.'

She reads me a section about terriers that would be familiar to any owner of a canine digging machine and proves that they've been showing their trademark behaviour for centuries.

She also tells me that Caius is rather scathing about dogs kept as pets by wealthy women, describing them as 'instruments of folly for them to play and dally withall, to trifle away their treasure of time, to draw their mind from more commendable exercises'.

One assumes he never shared those thoughts with Queen Elizabeth I.

Ciara explains that there are lots of breeds that arrive later, from the Continent, like the poodle, which was doing duck-hunting work right into the 18th century until the marshes were drained in Germany and they no longer needed dogs who could swim so well. Poodles were employed in the Russian army, in French circuses and all sorts of places because they were so intelligent and trainable.

The thought of poodles sparks something in Ciara's brain and she turns back to the library shelves to find me another treasure.

'My favourite thing here is about a poodle who got accused of witchcraft,' she says, producing a thin book of only a few pages, A5 size, dating from 1642. It has a marbled cover showing an ink drawing of a dog who looks like a lion.

'This is "Boy". He belonged to Prince Rupert of the Rhine, nephew of Charles I, who was taken hostage when he was a teenager during the Thirty Years' War and kept in Linz. His uncle, the Earl of Arundel, arranged for him to have a companion so he was given Boy, a local white hunting poodle.'

That's typical of the aristocracy. *Bad luck, lad, you've been taken hostage, but here you are, have a dog. That'll make you feel better.* When Prince Rupert finally came back to London, he came with Boy the white poodle.

'No one had ever seen anything like it!' Ciara says. 'With that colour and cut of hair. Prince Rupert was very well known as a fashionable, handsome young man, good at tennis and that sort of thing, with this amazing white dog who went everywhere with him. Come the outbreak of the Civil War, he is obviously a Cavalier general in the Royalist forces and Boy is still by his side.'

With the context set, she returns to the book, which is a Civil War propaganda pamphlet.

'This is the fake news of the Civil War period and what we see here is Boy being accused of witchcraft and, by extension, Prince Rupert is being accused of it as well.' So what could Boy do? According to the pamphlet, he had the art of prophecy, he could find concealed goods, he was imbued with the gift of languages, he was weapon-proof and he also had the power of invisibility. 'It also says he is aloof, seduces women, he hates prayers, he curdles custard,' continues Ciara. 'And finally, it says he is a "mere malignant Cavalier dog with something of the devil in or about him ... This is no dog, this is a witch."'

I am listening to this with my mouth open. This is some dog, I think. Maybe we should get a poodle? My American grandmother (my father's mother) had poodles and loved them. It would solve the hair allergy issue for Alice and they're renowned for being super-clever and obedient. We might even get one with Boy's extra powers.

Clearly, Boy had spooked the Roundheads with his intelligence and many talents.

'There's two ways to take this,' Ciara says, referring back to the pamphlet. 'It was taken at face value for a long time, but it is now considered more likely that it was counter-propaganda, so it could have been written by Prince Rupert and his pals as a mickey-take. It mocks the religious sensibilities of the more Puritan of the Parliamentarians. It's very funny and I think it's intentionally so.'

Whatever its intention in terms of target, the pamphlet raised Boy's status even higher, and possibly meant that he became a prize target. At the Battle of Marston Moor in 1644, Boy was killed in action.

'The lesson from this is don't take your poodle into battle,' Ciara says grimly.

Historians don't bother with softening the blow, do they? Poor Boy. Killed in action. He is the oldest dog on record at the Kennel Club library that has a name, an age, an owner and even a personality.

Bob starts barking, and I initially think it's because he has misheard the name 'Boy', but it's actually to announce the arrival of a visitor. Alice has made the trek from Piccadilly Circus and has survived. Bob greets her with his tail wagging.

'Oh hello, who are you?' Alice bends down to greet and admire him. 'You're lovely. What is he?'

'A Portuguese water dog,' Ciara and I say in unison.

Bob leans against Alice's leg and invites her to stroke his silky soft coat. Bob has a short haircut known as retriever cut, so he doesn't look like any Portuguese water dog you would see in the show ring with big hair at the front and shaved back legs.

I wonder about the difference of coat type in dogs. They seem to have a far broader range than, say, horses or cats.

'Dogs have the most plastic morphology of any mammal,' Ciara says, as I make a mental note to memorise that line so I can repeat it with authority to impress people. She goes on to explain that this means they have the most variety in appearance, in size, in coat type, because they've been bred to do so many different functional tasks for upwards of 25,000 years.

The Kennel Club library is, on the surface, a literary museum about dogs, but it's also a treasure trove of information about people.

Knowing that Alice won't be thrilled if I make her look at all the paintings and dog statues in the gallery, I ask Ciara to tell us about the calls she gets from people hoping to find photos or information about family members who had shown dogs back in the day. Alice likes a bit of family intrigue.

'I had some very nice people from Yorkshire who were trying to track down their grandfather who was a fox terrier exhibitor, so they were looking in catalogues for his name and maybe his photograph.' Ciara is warming to the task of telling Alice a good tale. 'They found him and they were triumphant about it. I asked whether they were into dog showing at all and they explained that no, they had no particular interest in dogs, but they were after proof of their grandfather's "other life" with his second family.'

That photo was of him with another wife and a new address. The man had ditched his first wife and all their children, moved across the Pennines and married again without getting divorced. That meant he was committing bigamy, which was and still is illegal. You'd have thought it might have been a priority to keep himself incognito, but the lure of the show ring proved too much for him to stay out of the limelight.

The family who had come with the query were satisfied to find the proof they had been after that their grandfather had not died as they had been told, but had gone on to live a secret second life, with dog showing still very much a part of it.

Heidi Hudson – the proud owner of Bob – is Curator of Photographic Collections at the Kennel Club. Heidi tells Alice about a woman from Australia who was doing research on her birth mother who she knew had shown Dalmatians at Crufts. Heidi duly found the record of her entries into classes at Crufts, but sadly no photos because she hadn't won any prizes. She sent back the information she had and was thanked profusely by the Australian woman, who told her that dog showing was probably only a cover or a way of getting to a contact because her mother's main occupation was as an MI5 spy.

'Oh, FANTASTIC!' Alice says, her eyes lighting up. Her father worked for 'the Office' and never revealed exactly what he did. Her extended family always believed he was a spy-master like 'M' in James Bond, and no one wanted to dispel their glamorous assumptions. His job may actually have been rather more mundane, but we may never know.

Alice is now rather glad she came and is about to learn all about Charles Cruft.

'I didn't know the show was named after a person,' she says, and I wonder if I've never made that clear on TV; I think I have and she wasn't really listening.

I tell her to think of the Hugh Jackman character in *The Greatest Showman* and imagine a man creating The Greatest

Dog Show. I knew he had been a dog-biscuit salesman, but I wasn't aware of the breadth and depth of his marketing skills. Ciara tells us more:

'Charles Cruft worked for Spratt's [a dog-biscuit company] and went in as the office boy at about sixteen years old. He was running the place by the time he was twenty-six. They had just invented the modern dog biscuit and he was keen to flog them so he started Cruft's in 1891. Here's the programme from 1898.'

Alice starts flicking through the pages and sees the huge number of adverts for dog food, medication and bleach. If anyone thought marketing, sponsorship and advertising were modern inventions, think again. Charles Cruft was all over it.

'"Dogs grow larger and quicker: cod liver oil for both man and beast",' she reads. '"Puppy worm balls!" What are they? "This show is disinfected with Sanitas." Good to know.'

The Kennel Club also has an extensive collection of show catalogues. Many have had to be digitised because whatever glue and paper they were using in the 1970s and 1980s was rubbish. Before that, the catalogues were much better made; the 1860 catalogue for the first ever major all-breeds show in Birmingham is in excellent condition.

The catalogues contain the names and addresses of every competitor and the dogs they were showing. They show a huge geographical spread and a diversity of social class. There are also interesting trends in terms of who owns what.

Aristocratic women tended to show a large, exotic breed like a Borzoi, while a working man would be more likely to show an Airedale terrier. Toy dogs were almost exclusively owned by women, whereas the men dominated the list for gundogs.

The show catalogues are better than an annual Census if you want to get an idea of where people came from, which dogs they favoured and what products they were buying. Or at least, which products they were being encouraged to buy. Some of the canine medical remedies are at best fanciful and at worst deceptive. I suspect there was a lot of magic medicine being sold by fast-talking, sharp-witted salesmen.

Charles Cruft was no doubt the master of them all. He knew he needed the masses to make his show successful and so nearly everyone got a medal, a rosette or a certificate. He wanted people to enjoy taking part, to feel valued and to pay to come back again as participants and as spectators. He knew what he was doing, and Cruft's show rapidly became the most popular and highest-profile dog show in the world.

Nowadays the official brochure is not that much different – dog food, dog medicine, cleaning products, portrait artists and photographers, but add to the list grooming equipment, dental products, toys, clothes, beds, books on training and behaviour, boarding kennels and day care. There is big business in dogs and Charles Cruft was the first person to understand and take advantage of the financial opportunity.

On the way out, I make Alice look at some of the art and the many china and porcelain dogs.

She concludes that the Kennel Club clearly knows how to make and hang on to money, as this is a five-storey building just off Piccadilly in the centre of London and it's worth a fortune.

I think that's an odd take-away from a visit to the world's largest and most detailed collection of canine art and literature, but I happen to know that the Kennel Club at one time owned the freehold to several buildings on the street, so she's got a point. She also says:

'If you ever buy me a porcelain dog, I'm leaving you.'

CHAPTER 3

Dogs for Good, Oxfordshire

Alice and I are travelling up the M40 towards Banbury, on our way to visit Dogs for Good. It's generally better if I do the driving because we are both more relaxed that way. When she's driving I have to keep alert for potential hazards, encourage her to move into the fast lane, try not to be concerned that she's got so involved in a political discussion on the radio that she's inadvertently slowed down and the car behind is now flashing its lights, give clear and consistent instructions as to when to take the next turning like a human satnav but a bit quicker because sometimes the map isn't quite right and we end up in a Morrisons car park instead of the A1 north.

Alice doesn't like it when I try to get her to speed up to 70mph by clicking at her as if she's a horse. I've always thought it's a gentle and encouraging way to suggest that sitting in the middle lane at 65 is not going to get us there on time. Then there's the occasional 'ghost brake' where I press the imaginary brake on the passenger side of the car if I feel she needs to slow down or stop. Oh, and the encouragement to switch lanes to take a gap in a queue of traffic or pull out at a junction by waving my hand as if conducting an orchestra. Even I can see that taking me as a passenger might be quite annoying. At least she's now got an automatic car so I don't have to change gear for her.

'I'd like to point out I've never had a crash,' Alice says through gritted teeth. 'Or any points on my licence. Now STOP IT or get out.'

I cannot argue (for that would necessitate the car slowing down even more) so I sit there in a vexed state trying not to say anything at all.

When we arrive at Dogs for Good, we are going to see Labrador puppies in the very early stages of training and meet the full-grown article at the end of training, ready to go off to change someone's life by opening doors for them, switching on lights or unloading the washing machine by gently taking out clothes and putting them into a basket.

Alice has her inhaler with her, just in case the coughing starts.

* * *

Dogs for Good is a very impressive charity that breeds dogs (nearly always Labrador/golden retriever-crosses), houses them with volunteers who agree to the schedule of socialisation and training, and then pairs them with people or families who need help.

When Mount Vesuvius erupted in AD 79 and covered Herculaneum in volcanic ash and rocks, it preserved many of the buildings with murals still intact. There is one picture that depicts a man with a staff being guided by a dog on a lead, and it is thought to be the earliest representation of a guide dog. In Paris in the 1780s, dogs were trained to help patients at Les Quinze-Vingts, the hospital for the blind, and in the following decades there was work in Austria and Switzerland on training dogs to help guide those with visual impairments.

Later, during the First World War, thousands of German soldiers were blinded on the Front by wounds or gas and, when they returned home, a doctor called Dr Gerhard Stalling started to explore ways in which dogs might help. In August 1916 he opened the world's first guide dog school in Oldenburg, near Bremen in north-west Germany. The idea took off and over time many more such schools opened.

As always with these things, to go international you need both enthusiasm for the cause and money. An American living in Switzerland called Dorothy Harrison Eustis heard news of one of the dog-training schools outside Berlin and decided to visit. Having spent a few months there, she was so impressed that she wrote an article for the *Saturday Evening Post*, a popular magazine published weekly in the States. The subsequent correspondence persuaded her that this was an idea with legs, as it were.

She trained a German shepherd dog called Buddy to work with one of her correspondents, a young man called

Morris Frank, who then helped her take the methods and ideology back to America, with a school called The Seeing Eye. It was the first training establishment in the USA for guide dogs and it still exists today in Morristown, New Jersey.

Here in the UK, two women in Wallasey in north-west England heard about this new phenomenon for training dogs to help guide those who were visually impaired. They contacted Dorothy Harrison Eustis and she met them in London in 1930. Muriel Crooke and Rosamund Bond were both German shepherd enthusiasts, and with the help of a trainer sent over by Mrs Eustis, they took on seven dogs and once they had raised them to a sufficient level, introduced them to four blind men who were also trained.

One of those men was Musgrave Frankland, the Secretary of the Liverpool Royal Institute for the Blind. Having trained with a bitch called Judith, he took her home with him and six months later reported that she had transformed his life.

'A guide dog is almost equal in many ways to giving a blind man sight itself. Judith has been worth her weight in gold and I would not be without her for a day.'

So it was that the Guide Dogs for the Blind Association was founded.

* * *

Dogs for Good builds on that idea of dogs being able to transform human lives, but stretches its reach beyond the visually impaired. It started in 1988, supported by Guide Dogs, and in 2000 moved to its own base north of Banbury. They train about 50 dogs a year but also have a dedicated 'Family Dog service' which helps families with autistic children that might benefit from having a dog in their lives. That programme helps around 350 people a year. They also have a Community Dog service which involves expertly trained dogs, who live with their handlers, visiting people with dementia or mental health challenges. For example, one of their staff members is helping a woman overcome her agoraphobia by visiting the local supermarket with the support of a dog.

We are greeted by the new Dogs for Good CEO, Ed Bracher. He shows us towards his office, which I notice has a child gate across the door. All of the office doors have these gates, which of course are not for children, they are for dogs. We used to have one in our house to stop Archie rushing towards the front door. Lots of people use them to stop their dogs going upstairs or into certain rooms. I imagine these gates are to make sure the dogs don't wander out of important meetings because they're bored. There are tubs of dog treats on the desks in the office and a dog bed. There are toys strewn across the floor. It looks like a toddler's nursery but without the brightly painted walls.

Alice and I sip coffee as Ed explains the most recent mission of Dogs for Good, which is to train dogs to help people with dementia.

'I've seen dogs recognise the eleven o'clock alarm signal and collect the bag of pills that is needed at that hour,' he says.

'They will then take them to the person with dementia and lick them on the hand until they take the pills.

'At 2pm, when another alarm goes off, the dog will collect the yoga mat and motivate them to do their exercises.'

He explains that a dog owner will never get cross with a dog for nudging him to take his pills; I'm thinking of my father here, who will get annoyed at my mother for supposedly 'nagging' him to take them. If Boris were the one making him do it, he'd smile and obey. Sorry, that's a ridiculous idea. Boris would never be capable of telling my father to take his pills and would most likely eat them himself, but if he were a dog trained by Dogs for Good, my father might smile at him and obey the command.

The other benefit, of course, is to the carer who is often also the partner of the person with dementia. They have to take the dog for a walk every day and that gives them a vital escape. You can't feel guilty or selfish for going out if you're walking the dog. It gives the carer a precious break and often creates a network of friends who are fellow dog owners with whom you can discuss your daily problems – or not talk about them at all. No pressure.

'A natural support system is invaluable as we know that most people who are at home every day caring for a loved one become desperately isolated and lonely,' Ed says. 'It can turn into a daily routine of frustration and desperation without a regular escape.'

'I don't want to be glass half empty ...' Alice interjects, and I know what's coming.

I am permanently enthusiastic and positive, whereas she is much more sanguine. It's like living with an insurance broker who is always weighing up the worst-case scenario. To be fair, she goes on to make a very good point and one that I suspect you are thinking yourself:

'Presumably people with dementia can have anger-management issues, so you do have to be careful about that? You wouldn't want them losing their temper with the dog. That's just not fair.'

Yup. Good question. I have failed in my role as a researcher and she has picked up the pieces. Ed agrees that it's a hot topic.

'We had a meeting about this only yesterday and you're right, it is something we look at really carefully,' he says. 'What's really interesting is the impact of the dog on the partner and how attached they get. Often, if their loved one has to go into a care home, they keep the dog and take it in to visit. It's a comfort that their wife or husband always remembers the dog, even if they've reached the stage where humans are no longer recognisable.'

My father has Alzheimer's, so I am more than aware of this scenario. He is still able to identify the immediate family but it's the dogs he really cares about. For years, if not always, his *only* domestic duty was to feed the dogs and he was still in charge of that task until quite recently. He would sing as he made them a concoction of dog biscuits, leftovers and occasionally an egg. Pouring hot water to soften the biscuits, he would sing, 'Oh diggy dog digs, diggy dog digs, isn't this the best dinner you've ever had? Yes it is, diggy dog digs.'

I suspect Boris's digestive system is grateful for the simpler menu my mother provides, but it's amazing how much Mac and Boris loved my dad and how they would always go and find him to lie on the bed with him, or rush over to his chair when they came in from a walk to tell him all about it.

Back at Dogs for Good, Ed is explaining how the dog supply works. They have 12 active broods living with volunteers who care for them and are involved in the birth of the puppies. That seems like a rather wonderful job, constantly surrounded by puppies, except that just as they learn to be house-trained, you have to give them up. Also, as we know only too well, the birthing process can be traumatic.

I don't have any expertise in birthing puppies. That has always been my mother's domain. Anna Lisa has also overseen it many times, of course. I have, however, helped to deliver kittens. Well, I say help. I looked on as Alice did the work when Button gave birth to five kittens.

I saw myself as the media manager of this event, so when her waters broke, I started a WhatsApp group to share the news. Two hours later, nothing had happened. My brother called.

'Clarey Bow, I'm sure you think you know what you're doing but you'd better call the vet. She should've had the first kitten by now.'

I was touched (and surprised) by his interest. He never calls me. We see each other plenty but we don't 'chat'. Who does that with their brother?

Oh yeah, Alice does. Once a week she calls her older brother Rob and they catch up on their news. Hers is usually about golf and his is usually about triathlon or tennis. It's not deep, but it matters. She used to talk to her mother every single day whereas mine only calls when there's news to tell me. I try to phone just for a chat, but it doesn't really work. I guess we're not a chatty family.

So my brother had called me because he sensed a veterinary emergency.

At that very moment, Alice cried out, 'It's coming!'

I put the phone down, probably without saying goodbye.

'It's breech,' she said confidently. She had done a lot of online research and comes from a family of doctors, so is good at this sort of thing.

'I'm going to have to help it.'

'I thought we weren't meant to touch it …' I was starting to say, but as if she was in an episode of *Casualty* or *Holby City* (in both of which Alice has appeared) she was already delivering a baby.

Even if it was only acting, that experience gave Alice the confidence to be quick and decisive in the event of an emergency. She released the first kitten from its backwards position and it plopped out onto the carpet – don't worry, we had placed a large square of off-cut on top of the newly laid cream carpet – and didn't move. We both looked at each other in a panic.

What now? Button leant over to lick it and there was movement. Then it squeaked. The first kitten was out and it was alive. I went back to WhatsApp to update the group. My brother didn't call again – for about a year.

There were five kittens in total. We weighed them every day and watched them grow. I have never leaped out of bed with such eagerness as those weeks when I knew I could go straight into the kittens' room and let them climb all over me. It was bliss. One of the kittens went to live with Rob, so that's another thing they talk about during their weekly catch-ups.

Imagine having the joy of new-borns all the time! That's what the Dogs for Good 'stock-holders' do. They oversee the birth of the puppies and keep them for eight to ten weeks before they are welcomed in the home of 'puppy socialisers', who look after them for approximately 14–16 months. Both roles are voluntary and Dogs for Good covers the costs.

When the puppy is about 18–20 months old they start advanced training sessions which typically take four months, and then they are paired with a suitable family or individual. The matching process is hugely detailed and involved.

The press officer for Dogs for Good, Maddy Phelps, tells me that they're not 'fluffy robots'. She continues: 'They need a lot of looking after and they're still a dog. We have instructors who look after clients and trainers who look after the dogs. They have a conference to try and match the right dog with the right person. They talk about the dog's needs as well as that person. If it's a really affectionate dog, for example, but the client can't give that affection back then we won't make that match. The dog has to be happy in the situation as well as the person.'

* * *

Alice and I had timed our visit to coincide with a puppy socialising class and, my word, it was an absolute treat. There were five puppies in total and they gathered in a large circle with their puppy socialisers. Even at such a very young age you can spot which dogs will be naturally suited to their role and which will require a bit more time and guidance.

Four of the puppies were very excited to see each other and the ones that had been littermates recognised each other and couldn't wait to say hello. The first ten minutes was fairly chaotic, but there was one blond puppy called Schuey (named after Michael Schumacher) who sat quietly watching everything going on with a quizzical expression on his face.

He had an aura that was so calm: an almost zen-like quality. I went over to sit next to him and he gently said hello before sitting down again to watch the room.

'The thing about these games is that we do it little and often,' Helen the trainer said, before she showed the handlers how she wanted them to proceed. Each puppy would take a circuit around the room and the idea was to get it to walk calmly with the handler rather than bound up to every other puppy or jump up to people.

The training is reward based, so it is all about positive affirmation of good behaviour. There is no tugging on leads or shouting and certainly no smacking. The puppies love their food so good treats are essential, and I loved the way Helen kept the same tone with every dog and with every person. To be honest, it's as much about educating the handlers as the puppies.

'Try to stay upright as you walk. That's it,' she says, watching one of the handlers walk. 'Wait until the puppy stops pulling and then offer the reward. That's it. Well done.' Helen sounded a bit like Joyce Grenfell.

Schuey was the star of the show, even though he was the youngest. I felt quite proud of him, and I'd only just met him. Imagine how Jo, his puppy socialiser, must have felt. She'd had Dogs for Good puppies before, so she has a very good base of knowledge. She also has an older dog at home who is a bit more advanced and he has been teaching Schuey how to behave.

'We have a cat as well,' Jo told me, 'and Schuey wanted to play with her, but our other dog told him not to. When I say told him not to, I really mean it. He literally put his paw on Schuey's head as if to say "no, we don't do that". I think Schuey has learnt a lot from him.'

I'm picturing that scene and have to laugh. The older dog reaching out his paw and calmly telling the puppy, 'no'.

The skills dogs can learn are really advanced, but what they also do is change the dynamic and the conversation between family members. They create a point of focus that can alter behaviour. If I ask my dad how the dogs are, we can have a bit of a conversation. Ask him what happened at the races or in the cricket that day and he resorts to 'I don't remember.'

When we were young, my mother used to send the dogs upstairs to wake us. It was so much better than an alarm clock and loads of families find that a useful way of getting reluctant teenagers to get out of bed. For families with challenging children or kids with extra needs, it can be a game-changer to have a dog.

Through the Family Dog service, the team at Dogs for Good is doing a lot of work with families who have autistic children. As all dog lovers know, your dog is your companion, your non-judgemental best friend, the one who will listen to your problems and always be happy to see you. For a child with autism, a dog can do all of that and also help build confidence and life skills, and be a reason for getting out of the house. The dog can also sense when might be a good time to put their head on a knee and offer comfort. They can support the daily routine of waking up, getting dressed, going to school or going to bed at the end of the day. They can even help develop speech, because the child learns to talk or read to the dog; or motor skills, the muscle movements we use every day. They help a child walk further and cope with different terrain. They'll even help with getting up and down the stairs.

The Family Dog service runs workshops online and in person to prepare the parents so that they know how to support the dog as well as their child. They also give unlimited aftercare and support so that the relationship is always supported. Everyone is focused on making sure the dog is comfortable and happy, because if that part of the equation isn't right, then the whole relationship won't work.

I filmed a feature a few years ago with a mother and her non-verbal autistic child. They had recently brought a dog into their life and the transformation was remarkable. Her son connected with the dog immediately and wanted to hold on to the harness. As a mother, she could now give instructions to the dog and so get through to her son.

Suddenly, she had control, and her stress levels reduced because she knew she could stop her son running out into the road or lying down on the floor of a supermarket because she would tell the dog not to do that. Finally, they could do things together. She started to see signs of an emotional connection and the beginnings of language.

There are around 700,000 children and adults living with autism in the UK, and although having a dog won't be possible or practical for all of them, it's a really fascinating adaptation of the dog/human assistance model.

Back in the training classroom, we have moved from the toddlers in nursery to the early stages of primary school. Sara Smith has been with Dogs for Good for five years. She is in charge of dogs from 18–20 months onwards, taking them through the early stages of assistance training.

Sheldon is a big, handsome Labrador/golden retriever-cross who is on the autism scheme. He is naturally friendly and enthusiastic. He's only 18 months old and is three weeks into his programme. For the first five minutes he is very excited about being with new people, but as soon as the training starts, he focuses on Sara and what she wants him to do.

'He has the perfect temperament and character for our autism scheme,' Sara explains as Sheldon wags his tail and smiles at us both. 'We look for quite confident dogs, sociable dogs that are calm in all situations. It's very important for our children that when they might be anxious or stressed, the dog stays calm. The children take a lot from how the dog is responding and they love pressure so we make sure the dog knows how to rest their head with downward pressure for quite long periods of time. It helps the child feel grounded and secure.'

Sheldon starts his class with a gentle paw push because it's his favourite thing and he's very good at it. Sara sits in a chair and places a soft round pad on the ground. Sheldon starts wagging his tail. His excitement is palpable and at first he picks it up in his mouth. Sara takes it from him and places it back on the ground. He tries again. This time he lays his paw on the pad. She has a clicker in her hand which she activates when he does exactly the right thing and he gets a small biscuit in return.

You can almost see his brain working as he realises, 'OK, I get it. This is what you want me to do.'

Sara's voice remains absolutely steady as she asks him to sit and lie down. He keeps his eyes on her and then when she nods he comes forward to put his paw gently on the pad. The idea is that the dog will be able to select a book or a DVD for a child, put their paw on their knee to tell them to clean their teeth or help in other tasks involving selection or instruction.

'They're big, bouncy babies at this stage, so there's no point getting frustrated. You have to just stay patient and calm. It's important that the dog has a good bond with us so we spend a lot of time cuddling and playing and exercising them as well as training.'

After a few minutes Sara moves on to a nose nudge. She puts a length of masking tape on her leg and Sheldon comes forward to push it with his nose. This simple act of enquiry can be a valuable diversion if a child is feeling panicked. The nose nudge requires a bit of pressure but it's more like an enquiry to see whether the child is OK. The children won't need masking tape, of course, that's just a way of making sure the dog pushes in the same place each time.

Interestingly, all this is done without a verbal instruction. Later in the training, Sheldon will learn key words and how to respond accordingly. Sara says they could learn hundreds of words over time.

Alice and I used to be quite proud that we'd taught Archie to sit and give us his paw. Now that seems pathetically inadequate.

Sheldon's final lesson is to lay his head on Sara's knee with downward pressure. She lays a tea towel on her knee and Sheldon moves forward to place his head on it. He is wagging his tail throughout. When he's been there for five seconds, the clicker goes off and she rewards him. The timings will increase and eventually he'll have his head there for ten or twenty minutes. He may even fall asleep in that position.

'I want him to enjoy it too, so if he relaxes and puts his whole weight on my knee, that's perfect,' Sara says. 'They get as much out of it as the child does and often they will seek them out if they think they need a bit of comfort and rest their head on their arm or their leg.'

The training session ends after 20 minutes with a game and a toy. It's always important to finish on a positive, fun note.

I'm starting to think that I might want to come back as Sheldon in another life. He's had the best time and he wants to learn so much. It's positively joyful to watch.

The dogs wear a harness when they are out and about, which acts as a warning to other people not to distract them and works as security for the children because they have something to hold on to. It also lets the dog know they are in professional mode. It's like putting on their uniform for work.

Sara says: 'A large part of the training is about safety, so making sure they sit at road crossings or at the top of the stairs without moving, even if the child tries to move. They learn left and right turns so that the team leader – usually Mum or Dad – can tell the dog which way to go and the child follows.'

As Sheldon departs the classroom, in comes the next pupil. He is Mason, a pale yellow Lab who sniffs us all and then sits in the centre of the room awaiting instruction. He is 20 months old and is on the physical training scheme. He looks like a young cadet at military school. Well fed, muscled up and ready for action. He will go into a home to help do things for a person who cannot physically do them for themselves, so he needs to be strong enough to pull open doors and drawers and pick up anything that needs lifting.

Sara sits in a wheelchair and drops things to the ground. It's important that the item is not a toy that they might have played with as a puppy.

A rubber dumbbell is dropped with some force and Mason doesn't flinch at the noise. He picks it up and gently places it in her lap. He does it again with a set of keys and then with a wallet. Each time the clicker goes off and he is rewarded with a treat.

'This dog will do anything for a biscuit,' Sara says. 'Biscuits make his day. He's been on a diet and he's managed to lose two and a half kilos so he looks really well now.'

Five minutes later he is pulling open the drawer of a chest of drawers with a rope and finally he works hard to learn how to take clothes out of a washing machine.

The last class of our visit is with Vernon, who is at the equivalent of A levels. He can respond to an alarm and collect medication, he can pull open big disabled toilet doors, and he can press buttons to open automatic doors. I suspect if he had to sit an exam he would pass with flying colours and cook the family a five-course meal to celebrate. This is one impressive and well-trained dog.

Again, it is clear that Sara's positive reinforcement training works wonders and that Vernon enjoys it. She always tries to finish the session with something he can do well and says that a dog will often come back having worked out what it was she was asking them to do in the last lesson.

'You literally see the light bulb go on,' she says. 'After a session like this, what they really should do is go home and sleep because they need to rest and take it all in.'

It's like teenagers, I guess. While I am marvelling at the brilliance of Vernon and the impressive nature of the training, Alice asks one of her 'reality check' questions.

'What happens to the dogs that don't make it? I don't want to say "fail", but you know what I mean?' she says, carefully.

Again, I have to concede, it's a good question. Life, as she keeps reminding me, isn't all roses, champagne and confetti. Where I constantly believe that one door closing means another one might open, she says that when one door closes, it's *shut* – don't embarrass yourself by tugging at the handle.

Now I can say, well, I wouldn't; I'd get Vernon to open the door for me.

The answer to the big question is that about one in five dogs will be withdrawn from the programme and often, it is for health reasons (allergies or joint problems) rather than behavioural issues. There is no shortage of welcoming homes for them to go to as a very well-trained pet. Lucky owners who get the most lovely, loyal and obedient dog who might occasionally open a door for them or do the washing.

The dogs work for about ten years with a client and then retire from active service. Although Dogs for Good officially retains ownership of the dog, the client will have the option of keeping them in retirement or allowing them to be rehomed. Friends, family members and sometimes neighbours will willingly take in the retired dog while the client gets a new working assistance dog.

The charity works on a budget of £30,000 per dog over its working life (that works out as just under £60 a week) and they will also provide financial support for clients who might need it so that pet food, insurance and veterinary costs don't prevent someone from having an assistance dog.

Before we leave, we meet Isabelle Atkins and Rumba. Isabelle is the Communications Officer at Dogs for Good. She came to know the charity through direct association because Rumba is one of their trained dogs. She credits Rumba with helping her graduate from the University of Warwick with a first-class degree in politics and complete a Master's in US foreign policy. I don't think Rumba wrote the essays for her, but maybe I'm wrong.

Rumba is very chatty and makes noises throughout our conversation, joining in with the discussion. Having always been dependent on other people to help her, especially her dad, Isabelle explains the impact this gorgeous, friendly and intelligent golden retriever has had on her life.

'It's transformative,' Isabelle says. 'From the moment I get up in the morning to the moment I go to bed, my life has a new purpose. I can now access the world independently. I can have a job – I wouldn't have dreamed of that before Rumba. It's completely changed the way I interact with people and given me a new outlook on life.'

Isabelle has a rare condition that means her joints dislocate easily, but Rumba can pick things up, take off clothes, help put them on, unload the washing machine and help her get out of the house, pressing buttons to call lifts or activate pedestrian crossings if required. The connection is not just about Rumba doing jobs that help Isabelle in a practical way; it's also about how she interacts with the world outside.

I know myself that being out and about with a dog is like having a special key that opens imaginary doors to friendship, but in this instance it seems even more magical.

'I am no longer invisible,' Isabelle explains. 'The questions have changed from "what's wrong with you?" or "why are you in a wheelchair?" Now they're about this amazing dog who is with me all the time who seems to have a golden halo around her.

'You can't go anywhere without people noticing Rumba and she is changing the way I can live my life. I am looking at moving into a flat on my own and I know I could never have done that without her being by my side to help me.'

On the way back home, Alice and I discuss what we've seen and learned. We decide that we might like to volunteer as puppy socialisers but then realise there's no way we could give a puppy back once we'd grown to love it. Nor would we be consistent enough as teachers. What we can do next time, however, is have a well-trained dog. On my travels around the UK, I will find out how to achieve that goal.

CHAPTER 4

Rescue Dogs, London

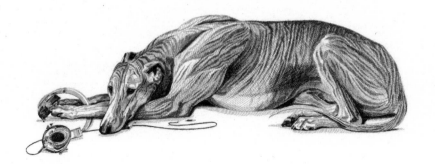

The oldest domesticated dog in the world is believed to be the greyhound. It is the only breed of dog mentioned in the King James version of the Bible, and also one of very few breeds to appear in both Chaucer's *Canterbury Tales* and Shakespeare's plays. You may already know that they are the fastest of all dogs, with a top speed of 40–45 miles per hour, but did you also know that they have been revered and celebrated for over 8,000 years? In Ancient Egypt, the greyhound was the hunting dog of choice for Pharaohs and their friends. When a favourite dog died, it would be mummified and placed in the family tomb of the wealthy and influential. The murals found inside the famous pyramids include images of greyhounds and the chances are that the Egyptian merchants on their travels took the breed across Europe and Asia.

There is even a greyhound saint. St Guinefort was his name, and he lived in 13th-century France. Legend has it that his master Guinefort had the greyhound guarding his baby.

A snake came into the room where the infant was in a basket on the floor, and threatened to attack. The greyhound sprang into action, killing the snake and saving the baby – but when the nobleman returned, he found the cot upturned and the dog with blood on his lips. He wrongly assumed that Guinefort had killed the baby, so he drew his sword and dispatched his own dog. Only then did he discover the baby perfectly safe behind the cot, and a snake covered in dog bites dead on the floor. He was consumed with regret so buried Guinefort under a pile of stones and planted trees in his honour. The grave became a shrine, and parents would take babies there if they thought they needed healing. Such was the perceived power of St Guinefort the greyhound that when the church found out he was a dog, they dug him up as a heretic. It is yet more proof that greyhounds have been influential figures in history and religion for thousands of years.

In honour of greyhounds, and to find out more about their character, Alice and I are heading across London to see our friend and fellow broadcaster Fi Glover. Fi is the guardian of a former racing greyhound called Nancy. I say guardian, because if you adopt a greyhound, you are never the 'owner', you are the adopter for life. Fi's son Hector also cooks a mean roast chicken which, given that neither of us can cook, only increases our desire to visit. We can put things in the oven, obviously, and we can boil vegetables, but we can't make a sauce or bake a cake. I'm even forbidden from following the HelloFresh recipes because Alice, who approaches them like a scientist, finds my own looser interpretations too free-ranging. Our lack of culinary expertise means that we are keen to go all the way to east London for fresh gravy and bread sauce.

Alice and I first met Fi decades ago at the BBC. I stood in for her on a Radio 4 programme called *Saturday Live* when she was on maternity leave and Alice, in her role as continuity announcer, frequently put Fi's shows on the air and introduced her with things like:

'And now on Radio 4 it's time for *Saturday Live* with Fi Glover.'

You have to read that in a Radio 4 voice, by the way. It doesn't work otherwise.

For many years, Fi and Jane Garvey presented a hugely successful podcast called *Fortunately*. The podcast revealed what I had always known about their respective personalities: Fi is a dog and Jane is a cat. Essentially, Fi will always wag her tail when she sees you, whereas Jane will either stick her tail in the air and walk away or, if you get too close, scratch you. Most people fall into one type or another, and I suspect there have been whole books written about just that concept.

We have also had dinner at Jane's house (admittedly self-invited) and I even arranged for her to adopt her cat Dora from a rescue centre in Hampshire. You'd think that might promote me somewhat in her affections, but no – Jane is steadfastly aloof – a true cat.

I bumped into her at Warrington Bank Quay train station in the autumn of 2022, when we were all switching routes because of various issues on the lines. I was coming back from the Rugby League World Cup finals at Old Trafford. She had been visiting her parents in Liverpool. I was delighted to see her and bounded up, as is my wont, to say hello.

'Oh God,' Jane said. 'Not you.'

This has happened many times, but like a puppy bothering an older cat who wants peace and quiet, I never learn. If Fi had been there, she might have put her hand on my head like that older dog with the Dogs for Good puppy and said, 'No, we don't do that.'

At least I knew enough not to try and sit next to her on the train.

* * *

We arrive in the wilds of east London and Nancy is the first one to the door. I can see her enormous shape through the stained glass with her nose against the letter box. The first thing that strikes you about Nancy is her size. She is huge. She is brindle in colour with a little grey around her muzzle. She is refined, sleek and incredibly muscular, with the thighs of a gymnast or a dancer.

'Wouldn't you want to have those muscles with only three and a half minutes of exercise a day?' Fi asks when we get inside. 'Because that's literally all she does. She does one pounding run when we go out but otherwise, if I try and walk her for more than forty minutes, she sits down. No stamina.'

It is a common misconception that big dogs need a lot of exercise, but it is all breed dependent. Greyhounds need short, sharp runs and then in fact spend most of the time sleeping.

We are taking Nancy for a (short) walk. When we reach a park, she is off the lead and galloping away to say hello to a whippet. Her stride is vast and when she takes off, the speed is electric.

'Isn't she beautiful?' says Fi. Alice and I agree. 'It's the most joyful thing. She runs like a cheetah. She is so fast and every single time it fills me with delight because it's like watching a proper wild animal taking off. It makes her so happy and she still has the timing in her so she does the equivalent of a circuit of the racetrack and then comes back. It's wonderful.'

Nancy returns with a huge grin on her face, tail and body wagging in delight.

Fi was on the waiting list for a greyhound for three years before Nancy became available at Whittingham Kennels in Waltham Abbey. She was six years old.

'I took one look at her and she took one look at me and I just knew,' she says.

Nancy had been entered for a few races but, according to her records, didn't finish them.

'That's typical Nance.' Fi laughs. 'Why bother?'

She was quickly retired from racing. She had a litter of puppies at the kennels and was the wet nurse for other puppies because of her lovely temperament and her maternal instinct.

'They're really gentle animals. Beautiful, calm and lovely.'

Given her size, it is a good thing she is gentle. She must measure about two metres from her nose to the tip of her tail.

One of the issues with racing greyhounds is that they don't know their name, because they've always been part of a pack, so their recall is non-existent. Fi had to work hard to train Nancy to recognise her new identity. It's not as easy with a breed that is not that motivated by food, so how do you train a dog who doesn't want treats?

'One of the things that tends to happen with rescue greyhounds is that they do become rather instantly devoted to you.' Fi smiles and almost blushes. 'Lots of owners say they develop a massive fixation with you, the human, because they've not really had that before. She did exactly that.'

Nancy confirms this theory as she comes galloping back again for a pat. There is no stronger reward than love.

In terms of challenges, there is an obvious issue with any dog that has only lived outside in kennels.

'She was "house trained", in inverted commas, but there's only so much training you can do with a dog that hasn't lived in a house,' Fi explains. She tells me that Nancy knew she shouldn't soil her bedding, but every other bare floor in the house was fair game as far as she was concerned. Nevertheless, she got used to it very quickly and since then, Fi says she has been as good as gold.

I remember as a child watching the Greyhound Derby with my grandmother and her sister, Aunt Ruth. It was live on the BBC quite late at night and I was allowed to stay up to watch. They told me about the background to the race, how it had started in 1927 and two years later a superstar called Mick the Miller had come along and won it by ten lengths in front of a crowd of more than 50,000 people at White City. He won the Greyhound Derby again the following year. In fact, Mick the Miller won 19 successive races before he was retired in 1932 to his owner's home in Kent.

His popularity helped greyhounds flourish in the 1930s, and well into the 1990s greyhound racing had general public support – the pop group Blur used a picture of racing greyhounds on the cover of their bestselling album *Parklife*.

I think all those who watched greyhound racing, me included, had no idea of the life some of those dogs were living. I assumed that it was similar to a racehorse and that they were treated like professional athletes – well fed, carefully and regularly exercised, living in luxury and personally nurtured. That may be true of the best kennels, but sadly there were too many cases where it was not. The injury statistics are frighteningly high, and the Greyhound Trust, founded in 1975, campaigns for the welfare of racing greyhounds, as well as finding homes for those who have retired.

For those who adopt greyhounds, or any other rescue dog, there are support groups of fellow adopters with whom you can share stories or seek advice.

'They're all lovely people and there's so much to talk about that is of very little interest to anyone else. Lots of conversations about recall, prey drive, arthritic back legs, very long chats about what can be eaten because they are very fussy, and then there's the wind.'

What? Why would you talk about the weather?

'No,' Fi says. '*Wind*. They have terrible wind. You've got to find the right feed for them, otherwise you can be asphyxiated overnight. Luckily the community is huge, so you can get answers to pretty much anything.'

You can also join up and go for walks together and Fi joined various 'hound groups' when she first got her but then realised that Nancy was happier on her own. She didn't really want to play like other breeds of dog. I wonder whether she might be projecting. Was that really what Nancy wanted, or was it what Fi wanted?

'Well, there may be some truth in that, because there were definitely times when Nancy just didn't want to talk about Brexit any more.' She laughs.

Nancy has had her few minutes of running and is ready to head home. Her head drops and she plods quietly along on the lead. She's had enough.

A few years ago Nancy had a scare when she ate a full pack of chewing gum which contained the sugar substitute xylitol, which is absolutely lethal for dogs. Even a small amount of this plant-based sweetener can cause hypoglycaemia, which leads to seizures and liver failure.

'I heard this rustling, 'Fi remembers with a shudder. 'And I saw the wrapping from a bumper pack of chewing gum strewn across the floor. I phoned the vet and explained what had happened and how much she had consumed. The advice was to take her straight to the emergency hospital and that's what I did. If I could have put a siren on my car I would have done.'

Nancy had her stomach pumped within an hour and was in hospital for three days as she had to be monitored. Greyhounds have a small stomach but a very large intestine, so things can take a while to work through and obviously chewing gum can cause a blockage – but the poisonous xylitol is a more major issue. I have heard cases of dogs eating only a small amount of a food containing xylitol and dying within days.

Nancy was very lucky and Fi says she can't even think about what might have happened if she had been out that evening and hadn't noticed what had happened so quickly.

When we get back to Fi's house, we meet the newest additions to her family, two kittens called Brian and Barbara. They are 12 weeks old. Brian is mainly white with a black saddle patch along his back and a black splodge across the top of his head, while Barbara is a ball of grey fluff with a nose that has been dipped in white paint and paws that are also white at the very ends. Alice immediately scoops her up for a cuddle.

One of the dangers with greyhounds is that, having been trained to chase a fluffy toy, they see everything with fur that moves as prey. Nancy's lack of instinct in that sense is a blessing. She lets Brian and Barbara and the older cat (who is called Cat) rule the roost.

We sit down for Hector's delicious Sunday roast. Excellent bread sauce, by the way. Not even made from a packet, which is what I would have done. Nancy is sprawled across the length of the sofa, pooped. She wakes up when she is offered leftover bits of chicken but lets the kittens take the first offering and backs off until they've finished. I've never known a dog like her.

Fi is so in love with Nancy that during lockdown in 2020, her children arranged a wedding ceremony for the two of them. In common with all of us, they were missing major social events so they decided to invent one. Fi dressed up in a black boiler suit with high heels, put on some make-up and did her hair. It's fair to say she entered into the spirit of it.

'We had a lovely ceremony where my daughter wore a minister's outfit. She had printed something off from the internet so we had proper vows. It was a slightly kooky event, I'll give you that, but all of us absolutely adore her and I like to think the union would be upheld in some kind of a law somewhere.'

I suspect there are states in America where their marriage would indeed be legal and binding.

On the benefits of adopting a rescue dog, Fi is evangelical.

'It's a beautiful karma because you know you have saved a dog from what I think is a horrible life and what they bring is a kind of gratitude with them, so it's a really lovely pet.'

* * *

The Greyhound Trust is one of many animal charities in this country, including the RSPCA (founded in 1824), Blue Cross (founded in 1897) and Dogs Trust (founded in 1891). There was clearly a growing awareness in the 19th century that animals, particularly dogs, needed protection and help. This coincides with the history of the most famous and well-established dog rescue centre in the UK. 'The Temporary Home for Lost and Starving Dogs' was founded by Mary Tealby in 1860 in Holloway, north London. Tealby was a supporter of the RSPCA and had become concerned about the number of dogs she was seeing suffering from lack of food and care.

When it was first established, *The Times* ran an editorial pouring scorn on the idea, accusing Tealby and her supporters of 'ridiculous sentimentalism' and suggested they had 'taken leave of their sober senses'. The renowned author and regular magazine contributor Charles Dickens helped change the tide of public opinion by writing in support of the home, and not long afterwards, Queen Victoria agreed to bestow royal patronage.

That commitment from the Royal Family has continued through Queen Elizabeth II and now Queen Camilla.

After Mary Tealby's death, the home moved to Battersea in 1871. A few years later, a donor gave a bequest of £500 (a huge amount of money in those days) on the condition that the home would take in stray cats as well. So it became a refuge for both.

More than 3 million dogs and cats have been helped by the centre and it's an extraordinary place to visit. Despite its extensive history it feels fresh, clean and modern. They can house 120 dogs on site in Battersea, each with their own kennel.

Battersea has a policy of never turning away a dog or a cat, and they don't discriminate. It's really easy to make judgements about why a dog has arrived at Battersea and we often assume the worst of the owner and the dog. Having been there and talked to so many of the staff, I have a greater understanding and appreciation for the variety of situations that may have led to dogs needing to be rehomed.

Sometimes an owner falls ill or dies, sometimes there has been a change in circumstances, a divorce or relationship break-up, a job relocation or maybe the children haven't adapted to having a dog in the house. There are all sorts of reasons why a dog might need a new home.

Interestingly, Battersea can track the ebb and flow of a cost-of-living crisis, for example, because their intake numbers will suddenly rise. Sometimes they will take in a dog because the owner has to move into rented accommodation that won't allow pets and they can't find a willing friend to adopt it, or because they simply can't afford to keep a dog any more.

Battersea has plenty of dogs that have come from puppy farms or been found abandoned. They also know a lot about the perils of buying dogs off the internet where no research has been done by the new owner into the suitability of the dog or by the breeder into the suitability of the family who are buying it.

Veterinary costs are often the reason that owners reach the difficult decision to take a dog to Battersea. It's a last resort, but it is a responsible one as they are giving their dog a chance of urgent treatment and the potential of a new life in a loving home.

'Brachycephalic' dogs (which literally translates as 'shortened head') like pugs or French and English bulldogs, if they have upper airway abnormalities, can suffer from brachycephalic obstructive airway syndrome, which necessitates expensive surgery or treatment. Consequently, many of them arrive at Battersea in need of veterinary care.

Sometimes a dog will have behavioural issues that have caused problems in the home. Whatever the challenge, each one has a plan tailored to their individual needs.

Staff and volunteers work as teams to look after each block of dogs so they have an 'ongoing observational model' and really get to know them well. They have a team of canine behaviour experts as well as a veterinary surgery.

When I visited the centre, I was so impressed by the site and by the people who work and volunteer there. I may be romanticising it a bit, but they all seemed to be smiling. There is no doubt about how much pleasure and pride they have in their work.

Not far from Battersea Park and the River Thames, space is limited in London and the kennels have expanded as far as they can. Consequently, Battersea has other sites in Old Windsor in Berkshire and Brands Hatch in Kent. It has 500 staff and more than 800 volunteers across the three centres.

The Tealby block is the intake centre at Battersea where the new inmates have a chance to settle in a calm environment. Each dog has a two-part kennel with a back room where they can have some privacy and quiet and a front section where they can see and hear what's going on outside and move about freely.

They have special scented oils, calming music and the volunteers even sit and read to them to help the dogs relax. They have underfloor heating and plenty of natural light and air.

There are photos on a 'Happy Board' of dogs with new owners in their 'forever homes'. The emphasis on success stories reinforces the message that if you can make the right match, the story can always end happily.

Every dog is given a chance, because Battersea is non-judgemental and open-minded.

The centre manager, Becky MacIver, clearly loves it at Battersea. 'I've been working in animal care and welfare since I was fifteen years old,' she told me on my visit. 'There's a certain kind of magic when you walk through the doors here. I feel what the organisation stands for, its history and what the team do here, makes it very special.'

She also explained the process of finding the right people for the right dogs:

'When a dog first comes into us we take a full history from the owners. Sixty-four per cent of dogs are gifted into us by owners, so we can get a lot of information and that's crucial. We let the dog settle for a couple of days because it can be really stressful coming into a kennel for the first time. Once they're a bit more comfortable, the team gets to know them with ongoing observation. Every single day they're making notes on how they react to everything, what they like to play with, what sort of treats they like, what their personality is like.'

That way, the team has a really clear understanding of what sort of home and what sort of person will suit each dog. Every dog will be neutered and will have any required veterinary treatment before they are offered for rehoming. Then the matching process can start. The team at Battersea draws up a 'rehoming criteria' to work out what sort of home will be best for each dog.

They ask questions like: Will it be best in the country or in a town? Does it need to be with other dogs or on its own? With or without children? With cats or not?

They can then talk to the people offering to rehome and find out what sort of life they lead, how active they are and what they want from a dog before they let them meet to see if they feel that special connection.

Nathalie Ingham is the canine behaviour and training manager at Battersea. I asked her about how dogs can adapt.

'You see some dogs who have been through some really tough times and yet they are so forgiving. Regardless of what has happened to them before, they trust humans again and put all their faith in us as their new carers and their new family. That always amazes me, that you can come from a difficult situation and yet be transformed.'

We live in a world where the internet can give us answers to anything and can also present us with goods delivered to our door at the click of a button. There are many benefits to the immediacy of supply to demand but in terms of buying or adopting a dog, the fast track is not always the best track. Nathalie says:

'There are so many different places you can get a dog nowadays and it can be very easy to do it online, so you can suddenly wake up one morning thinking "I'm going to get a dog today" and by the end of the day you've got one. But you've got to think about the long-term commitment. You've got to be prepared financially and with your time.'

If you go to Battersea, you will not go home with a dog that day. Far from it. Nothing will happen straight away, but the reward for patience is that you get a chance of a relationship that will last for life. Most dogs live for, on average, 15 years so it's worth putting in the time before the relationship starts.

'Coming to a rescue centre means that you can find a dog that actually fits your needs,' Nathalie explains. 'If you want a dog that sleeps all day long, we can find you a dog that loves to live like that. If you are a keen runner and you want a companion that can get you out of the house to convince you to go for a five-mile run, we can find you that dog.

'That's the thing that rescue homes can do that doesn't happen anywhere else. We can find the right dog for the right people.'

* * *

There is a growing trend of adopting street dogs from countries where they roam outside. I understand that it is always done with good intentions, and I know the vast majority of those dogs will get far more care, affection and attention in their new homes, but it does concern me, both in terms of animal welfare and in the sense that, sometimes, we are imposing our ideas onto other cultures and judging them for not doing it the way we do.

When Alice and I travelled to India, we saw very healthy-looking dogs living in villages where people live very basic lives and have just about enough to feed their kids. They explained that they always make sure they have enough to feed the dogs and that they are treated with reverence and respect. They may not live inside and sit on the sofa, but that doesn't mean they aren't loved.

Of course, this is very different from dogs who are mistreated or abused and there are plenty of those, sadly, here in the UK. The charities who rescue them are very strict about the homes they will allow those dogs to go into and – not surprisingly – reject more offers than they accept.

That is sometimes the reason that well-meaning folks who want to rescue have to resort to the internet. They can find themselves paying a large amount of money to get a dog shipped over from abroad. As I say, I know it's done with good intentions but it can be hugely discombobulating for a dog to be wrenched from its familiar environment, shipped overseas and stuck in a strange house with people it has never met trying to pet it every day.

It's why early socialisation of puppies is so important, both with other dogs and with humans. If a dog hasn't had that experience, it will take months, sometimes years, to adapt. I also know vets are concerned that there is seldom a vaccination history with street dogs and they are fearful of diseases being spread amongst the dog population.

I respect anyone taking on that challenge, but I know from those I've talked to and dogs I have met that it is not straightforward and only works if you have time, space and an inordinate amount of patience.

As one of the success stories, there is a wonderful rescued street dog called Kratu who used to perform agility at Crufts. I say 'perform' because he really was a comedy performer. Rather than leap over a show jump, he would pick up a pole in his mouth and run around with it. He would wander off into the crowd and very much do his own thing. Along with everyone in the arena, I loved him, and he became a YouTube superstar. When I got the chance, I invited him and his owner Tessa Eagle Swan into the studio.

She told me that he is a very special dog but even he had taken a lot of work. There are no easy fixes. She had to respect him and learn to understand him. They've found their magic and he has changed her life.

It is a sad fact that 20 per cent of Battersea's intake are dogs that have been bought online. The decision to purchase would have been heavily influenced by looks or aesthetics, rather than personality or breed traits. Perhaps not surprisingly, the reality of owning that dog has not lived up to the expectation.

Battersea and the many other rescue centres around the country are doing their best to educate people to appreciate older dogs and to always value personality above all else.

Mary Tealby started her rescue home for lost and starving dogs in the same decade that Professor Philip Howell suggests that the idea of pet dogs living in the home became a regular occurrence. We now live in an age with more pets than at any stage in history, and more dogs needing help than ever before. Not everyone has the space, the time or the commitment to give a rescue dog a home, but those who do are gold-star dog lovers. As Fi Glover says, 'Everyone who takes in a rescue dog has that kind of warmth about doing it, but we get back so much.'

There is no doubt that adopting a rescue dog is an option for me and Alice to consider. There is much to discuss.

CHAPTER 5

Dogs and the Royal Family

The Royal Family has always included dogs. Henry VIII may not have been loyal to his wives, but he certainly was faithful to his dogs. In fact, he had a whole Royal Household department called The Kennels. As well as hunting dogs, he had pet dogs who wore velvet collars to mark them out as his special companions. His two favourites were called Cut and Ball, and when they went missing, he offered a significant reward for their safe return.

His son, Edward VI, had his life saved by the barking of his spaniel who was sleeping with him when Thomas Seymour attempted to kidnap the young King in 1549. The dog paid for his warning with his life, as Seymour killed him, but nevertheless the alarm was raised, the King was saved and Seymour was executed two months later.

Later, in 1615, King James I, with his son Charles, Prince of Wales, visited Cambridge University to attend a debate on 'Whether dogs could make syllogismes' – in other words, are dogs capable of combined reasoning? The subject had been chosen to suit the King's interests. John Preston of Queens' College argued that a hunting hound chasing a hare had to anticipate which way the hare might turn and make the correct choice to intercept the beast. The King is reported to have enjoyed the discussion and to have supported the notion that dogs did have the ability to reason.

When his son ascended to the throne, Charles I continued the family tradition of keeping dogs. He favoured toy spaniels, which became known as King Charles Spaniels as a result, and the Royal Collection shows a very touching portrait of his three eldest children with two spaniels affectionately leaning into their legs. Of course, the reign of Charles I ended in tragedy, and on 30 January 1649, the day of his execution, he was allowed one last walk in St James's Park with his pet dog before he was taken to be beheaded.

In 1660 when King Charles II restored the monarchy, he came with a full retinue of spaniels and always had two or three of them at his heels. The cavalier King Charles spaniel was named in his honour. Through the generations, dogs of various size and character have played their part in royal history.

* * *

Remember the film scene from the Opening Ceremony of the London Olympics in 2012? You know, the one where Daniel Craig as James Bond goes to Buckingham Palace to collect the Queen for her mission. A black cab deposits Bond at the front entrance and he skips lithely up the red-carpeted staircase. Two corgis run down the stairs to greet him and one of them rolls onto its back, showing off a trick he has performed all his life.

We see the back of the monarch's head and we all expected Helen Mirren or maybe Imelda Staunton to turn around as the Queen. James Bond waits patiently and then coughs gently. The figure in a pale pink dress turns round and a packed Olympic stadium, to which this was being played on the big screens, as well as the millions watching around the world, let out a collective gasp.

None of us expected it to be the *actual* Queen. It was such a closely guarded secret that even members of the Royal Family didn't know the Queen had filmed it.

'Good evening, Mr Bond,' she says.

Not only was Her Majesty the real deal, so were the dogs. Monty, Willow and Holly all featured and no canine stand-ins were needed for this film. I know that to be true because as the Queen rose from her chair to go with Mr Bond, the dogs didn't just trot along with her, they led the way.

How do I know? Well, I'd seen it for myself.

* * *

I first met Queen Elizabeth II when I was a young child. My father trained racehorses for her and as a gift to my parents when I was born, the Queen provided the pony on which I learned to ride.

She was a rotund, hairy little Shetland pony called Valkyrie. Not only did I learn to sit on Valkyrie, I also learned to fall off her, which is perhaps the more important lesson in life. Valkyrie lived until she was nearly 30 years old and whenever the Queen visited Kingsclere to inspect her racehorses, the fat little Shetland pony would be at the end of the line-up of sleek thoroughbreds. It was a comical sight and always made the Queen laugh.

Valkyrie was a pony who knew her own mind and – a bit like the corgis – could not be relied upon to behave herself, but would always raise a smile.

Over the years, I met the Queen many times at home, at the races and at various Jubilee or birthday celebrations. In June 2016, I compered the pageant that took place on the Mall for the Queen's 90th birthday. It was called The Patron's Lunch and was an eccentric and energetic parade of more than 600 charities for which Her Majesty acted as patron. It was billed as a street party and people had picnics on a typically damp London day.

At the end of it all, the Queen was scheduled to give her one and only speech of the birthday celebrations. I was standing on a small stage at the Wellington Arch end of the Mall, speaking into a microphone. I told the crowds what was to happen and stepped back as the royal party came onto the stage.

Along with the Queen and the Duke of Edinburgh were Prince William and his wife Catherine, Prince Harry and their cousin Peter Phillips, who had orchestrated the whole event.

The route up was a set of steps with fairly rickety banisters. I had a sudden moment of panic that the Queen might trip up the steps and wondered what on earth the protocol was for helping her to her feet. I held my breath as she walked up the steps unaided and without using the banisters. Not far behind her was the Duke of Edinburgh. As she got to the top, the Queen looked at me and said, 'Oh, it's Clare. How nice to see you here. Thank you for coming.'

Now, I know the rules about curtseying and saying Your Majesty and all that but in the heat of the moment it's easy to forget. I rushed into a rather clumsy bob and mumbled, 'Yes. Well. You're welcome. Lucky it stopped raining.' I paused and suddenly remembered the protocol. 'Your Majesty,' I blurted out.

She smiled as she must have done millions of times at people speaking nonsense in her presence. She must have spent her life wondering why the British population was so lacking in fluency. It was always helpful if there was a dog or a horse around to distract attention and calm the nerves.

The Queen gave a short and very funny speech in which she thanked everyone for coming out to celebrate and finished with the stern observation that enough was enough: 'How I will feel if people are still singing "Happy Birthday" in December remains to be seen.'

Her family laughed, the crowd cheered and all was well with the world.

* * *

Not too long before London 2012, I was invited for lunch at Windsor Castle. It was only a small gathering: no more than ten or twelve people in total. I drove to the ancient entrance and chided myself that I hadn't had my car washed. I had expected to be parked in a far-off car park, well out of vision, but instead I was sent through the fortified gates of the oldest and largest occupied castle in the world. I felt that familiar flutter of nerves.

I parked in the quadrangle as instructed, and was shown up to the drawing room where the assembled guests stood nervously sipping on pre-lunch drinks. I drank water and tried not to gulp, fearful of needing to go to the loo at the wrong time. I don't remember if a servant banged a stick on the floor but the atmosphere in the room changed and every-one stopped talking. We looked towards the door.

In trotted three corgis, followed by the Queen and the Duke of Edinburgh. The Queen moved amongst the guests, chatting easily and asking everyone what they had been up to and how their journey had been.

Again, I don't know whether a signal was given, but suddenly the corgis started to make their way towards the door. I was next to the Queen so followed her lead and we went out into the long, narrow corridor.

Windsor Castle has been home to 40 monarchs, dating back to William the Conqueror, and although it has been modified in that time, it is a place that oozes history. Paintings and suits of armour decorate the walls and there is much to take in, but any sense of grandeur was completely dissipated by the scene I witnessed as the corgis trotted ahead of the Queen, one of them playing with a small toy.

'Do they know where they're going?' I asked.

'Of course they do,' replied the Queen. 'They also know if we're late.'

We picked up the pace, and when we got to the dining room, the Queen sat at the head of the table and the corgis arranged themselves around the royal ankles. I suspect that a few things always 'fell off' the table into their mouths.

I sat next to the Duke of Edinburgh, who drank a glass of pale ale with his lunch. As everyone finished their starter, he was deep in conversation with a surgeon about her work.

'Philip!' came the familiar voice from the opposite end of the table. 'Bell!'

'Oops,' he said, and he pressed a small button on a disc that looked like a coaster.

Immediately the door opened and staff appeared to clear the plates. It was like a device Q might have provided for James Bond. I was intrigued.

'Sir, why doesn't the Queen have her own button?' I asked.

He looked at me with those famously pale, penetrating eyes.

'I've got to be in charge of some things,' he said with a twinkle.

I'm not sure the duke was particularly fond of the corgis. He preferred a practical gundog that would obey instruction and fulfil a function.

I thought it said a lot about the Queen's sense of humour that she had chosen such a stubborn and often unbiddable breed as the Pembroke Welsh corgi. The corgi is the most well known of all the Welsh breeds and is thought to have been brought over by Scandinavian settlers in the 11th century who used them for herding cattle. The name derives from the Celtic 'cor', meaning dwarf, and 'gi' meaning dog. They have short little legs, long bodies and bags of personality. There are two distinct types of corgi: the Cardigan and the Pembroke. The Cardigan is longer in the body, has slightly bowed front legs and a long tail. They have erect ears with tips that are slightly rounded. The Pembroke is slightly smaller and has straighter front legs. Traditionally, they had docked tails; since docking has been banned, some breeders have worked to produce dogs with natural bob tails.

The Queen's first Pembroke Corgi, Susan, had been a gift from her parents for her 18th birthday and began a life-long affair with the breed. Courtiers would often be seen walking them in the grounds of Windsor Castle and Bucking-ham Palace or lifting them up the steps of an aeroplane, into a train or into a car. If the Queen was on the road and it was practical to do so, the corgis went with her.

Her Majesty also cross-bred her corgis with her sister Princess Margaret's favoured dachshunds to create a 'dorgi'. These were equally roguish in behaviour. She owned more than 30 corgis and dorgis in her lifetime.

Dogs and the Royal Family

There is a cracking photo of England's rugby union World Cup-winning squad of 2003 sat with the trophy and the Queen. In the foreground is a corgi called Berry, photobombing for fun.

To investigate the history of the Royal Family and dogs, I again visited the Kennel Club library. Apart from Bob, no one else is in the library and I am free to roam the shelves.

There are all sorts of books on different breeds, books on showing, breeding, care and behaviour, as well as law, art and animal rights. On the wall by the reception desk is a striking modern photograph of a white Hungarian puli galloping out of the canvas, corded hair flowing in every direction. This is one of the more recent examples of impressive dog photography, and you won't find a better collection in the world than here at the Kennel Club.

The photographic collection runs to over two million images. Yes, that's two million pictures of dogs. It's a staggering amount and Heidi – a self-declared 'nerd' about photography – is always on the lookout for rare images, scanning eBay on her days off to find things that others may have overlooked. Her office is neatly arranged with boxes of catalogued photographs and, more importantly, a dog bed under the desk, a basket of dog toys and a couple of jars of biscuits for Bob.

Heidi shows me a photograph that was reproduced many times as a postcard. It shows the funeral of the Queen's great-grandfather, King Edward VII, in 1910. The streets are lined with mourners – the crowd was estimated at over three million – and it was the largest gathering of European royalty ever. It was also the last such assembly, as many of them were either deposed or executed in the following decades. Nine kings and even more queens, princes and princesses. However, all of them had to play second fiddle to a dog called Caesar.

A page from *National Geographic* magazine shows an aerial shot of the procession. A team of eight King's Troop horses are pulling the gun carriage and directly behind it are the King's favourite horse (saddled but riderless) and, behind him, Caesar the wire fox terrier being led by a Highlander. In terms of rank, the dog is officially the second most important mourner behind a horse. The text beneath confirms that impression: 'Caesar, the favorite (sic) dog of King Edward VII of Great Britain, marching before the foremost Kings and Princes of the earth in the funeral procession of his master.'

Some heads of state were said to be most put out that they were behind the dog in the pecking order, but the King had apparently left clear instructions.

Caesar had been the King's loyal and trusted companion since 1902 and wore a collar with a metal tag (now in the Kennel Club collection) engraved with I AM CAESAR. I BELONG TO THE KING.

Dog experts may tell you that he was not the best example of a wire fox terrier, nowhere near as fine as Blanca, who won the Terrier group at Crufts in 2023, but that is not the point. Edward VII adored him and spoiled him rotten, taking him with him on holidays to France, feeding him titbits from the table and confiding in him every day.

Caesar is immortalised in stone at the feet of his master on his tomb at St George's Chapel in Windsor.

Edward VII's mother, Queen Victoria, was also a renowned dog lover who acquired an extraordinary range and number of dogs. Heidi brings me a list of all the dogs Queen Victoria owned – it runs to 16 pages. There are hundreds of dogs.

There are about 200 staghounds listed and plenty of other dogs that would have been kept in outdoor kennels and used for hunting, such as bloodhounds, beagles and deer-hounds, but the breeds that catch my eye are the unusual ones. There are two truffle dogs named Daisy and Fairy, two Bedouin dogs called Stewart and Zohrah, three Cuban dogs, various spitzes, Pomeranians and a volpino Italiano ('volpino' translates as 'little fox'). Also quite unusual is the listing of three Esquimeaux, now known as Canadian Eskimo dogs.

Heidi explains that Queen Victoria's subjects were busy travelling the world expanding the Empire and they would come home with dogs from the lands they visited. That is how the Queen came to acquire so many exotic breeds. She would have been one of the first people in the British Isles to have a Pekingese – looted from the Summer Palace in Peking during the Second Opium War and consequently named 'Looty'.

Poor Looty had been part of the Imperial Family in Peking, warmly cherished by the Empress and carefully fed a diet of chicken and rice. Captain John Hart Dunne referred to her in his diary as 'a pretty little dog, smaller than any King Charles ... People say it is the most perfect little beauty they have ever seen.'

Little Looty had to survive the long sea journey back to Britain, personally tended to by Dunne, who presented her to the Queen in the hope that she would become a beloved pet for a second Royal Family. As it was, she did not adapt to the change in diet and turned her nose up at standard dog food. She was demoted to the kennels at Windsor Castle and spent the rest of her years there.

Looty was just one of the canine 'treasures' brought back from lands afar.

'It was the imperial age, it was the colonial age, and people were gifting her dogs from the lands they visited and conquered,' Heidi explains. 'So all these people were bringing back dogs from around the world as souvenirs.'

Even if she was collecting dogs as trophies, Queen Victoria was genuinely fond of them and the best evidence of that is found in the photos that Heidi has collected. She has a selection of *carte de visite*, small cards which were widely published and sold to the public as postcards. The one she wants to show me became a record bestseller. It is of Queen Victoria and her favourite Scotch collie, Sharp. Or perhaps I should say Sharp the first, as the Queen was not that inventive with names: she repeated the name Sharp for a further six collies, used Noble five times and Waldina for seven different dachshunds.

The original Sharp was a particular favourite.

'After Prince Albert died, Queen Victoria went into mourning at Balmoral and wasn't seen or heard of for years,' Heidi says as we look at the photo. 'The public were understandably concerned, and there were rising fears of a reaction against the monarchy. So a decision was made to do a photo shoot and to share images of the Queen.'

The Queen is wearing a wide black skirt, black jacket and a bonnet, one black glove and one bare hand holding Sharp around the shoulder. The dog is black with a white chest and a flash of white on his toes. He is sitting on a chair with his head leaning into her midriff as the Queen looks into the distance. There's emotion and intimacy in the photo, something you don't really associate with Queen Victoria. There are various different images and in all of them you can feel the connection between dog and human. I suppose one might call them sentimental.

'They were taken by a very famous photographer at the time.' Heidi points to the engraved letters of W. & D. Downey. 'There had never been a photograph of a member of the Royal Family, or indeed a celebrity, with this kind of intimacy. She's holding the dog, hugging it and – in one photograph – looking lovingly at it. It was something incredibly new and it became a massive hit with the public. It was the most sold *carte de visite* at the time.'

Heidi tells me that the photo was a means by which the Queen could connect with her public and also convey the aspirational Victorian values of virtue, honesty, fortitude and patience. All the things that might take a thousand words to be described in the poetry or novels of the time were encapsulated in this photo.

The *carte de visite* of Queen Victoria and Sharp the collie becoming a hit was the equivalent of an Instagram photo with a million likes, and much as an Instagram photo can start a whole new fashion, so these photographs popularised the notion of families or individuals posing for the camera with their dogs.

Queen Victoria's first dog was a cavalier King Charles spaniel called Dash, who has been referred to as her closest childhood companion. At the age of 13, she wrote in her diary that she had dressed Dash 'in a scarlet jacket and blue trousers'. A portrait of Dash by Sir Edwin Landseer was given to the then Princess Victoria by her mother as a 17th birthday present in 1836. Dash is buried in the grounds of Windsor Castle with the epitaph:

HIS ATTACHMENT WAS WITHOUT SELFISHNESS,
HIS PLAYFULNESS WITHOUT MALICE,
HIS FIDELITY WITHOUT DECEIT,
READER, IF YOU WOULD LIVE BELOVED AND DIE
REGRETTED, PROFIT BY THE EXAMPLE OF DASH.

Queen Victoria's union with Prince Albert was famously blissful and no doubt benefitted from their mutual love of dogs. In fact, Prince Albert's greyhound Eos joined them on their honeymoon in 1840. One assumes that Queen Victoria was happy enough with the arrangement, as she commissioned Landseer to paint Eos and gave it to Prince Albert as a Christmas present in 1841. It hung proudly in his dressing room at Buckingham Palace.

Queen Victoria may have started the trend for dogs being part of the household, treated as members of the family rather than working animals, but Heidi's star rating for royal dog owners is reserved for Queen Alexandra, the daughter of the King of Denmark and the wife of Edward VII.

'Queen Alexandra was very passionate about photography and took her own pictures,' Heidi says. 'I think she was the most "doggy" of all the royals. She started the LKA, the Ladies Kennel Association, and was really instrumental in making sure that women could show dogs. She had dogs her whole life and a lot of them were companion dogs.'

The Kennel Club was a male-only club. The Prince of Wales (later Edward VII) became its first royal patron. Ten years later, his wife formed the LKA and asked Queen Victoria to become its patron. If you're going to make a statement, that's not a bad trump card to play.

In terms of showing, Queen Alexandra's most successful dog was a beautiful borzoi called Alex. The elegant Russian wolfhound had been a gift from her brother-in-law, Tsar Alexander III, shortly before his death from kidney disease. Alex won a hundred first prizes and seven championships, including at one of the earliest Cruft's.

One assumes that the judges were fully focused on the pedigree of the dog rather than the owner. Alex became quite a celebrity in his own right, and his fame grew with photographs of him with the then Princess of Wales. Queen Alexandra went to the dog shows in person and was hugely influential in giving them status and increasing their popularity.

One could argue that dogs have played a key role in making the Royal Family relatable to the British public. From Charles I and his spaniels or his children arranged around a huge mastiff in the famous painting by Anthony Van Dyck, to the current Prince and Princess of Wales with their family dogs, nothing goes down so well as a picture of a royal with a dog.

Heidi says: 'I believe dogs have been a real connection for the Royal Family to their public. That idea of "we love our dogs too". That's really unique about the British Royal Family, and even today people are really happy to see William and Kate walking or hugging their cocker spaniel. It's very relatable.'

King Charles and Queen Camilla are both committed dog lovers and have broken new ground by adopting two Jack Russell terriers from Battersea. Beth and Bluebell are the cheeky-looking rescue dogs who have stolen their hearts. The then Duchess of Cornwall explained how she came to adopt them in an interview for Radio 5 Live.

'Along I went to Battersea,' she said. 'And Beth appeared. She had just been moved from pillar to post and dumped. We thought it would be nice for her to have a friend. They found Bluebell two or three weeks later, wandering about in the woods with no hair on her, covered in sores, virtually dead, and they nursed her back to life and her hair grew again. She's very sweet but a tiny bit neurotic, shall we say.'

I'm not surprised she's neurotic, given that start in life, and I suspect Queen Camilla has had to be extremely patient with her, offering comfort and consistency at every turn.

In a similar way to Queen Victoria and Queen Elizabeth II, it is the photos of the new King and Queen with their dogs that have connected with the public.

Their 15th wedding anniversary in 2020 was celebrated with a new photograph of them with Beth and Bluebell sitting on their knees. Although the official photograph was lovely, I particularly enjoyed the 'outtake' photo with King Charles laughing as he lifts one of them into the air in a desperate attempt to control her.

There is always, with dogs, the opportunity to show a more relaxed, fun side to your character.

Queen Victoria may have set the trend for dogs being treated as part of the family, but through the generations, members of the Royal Family have continued to understand that there is a deep emotional response from their subjects to that bond.

During the concert to celebrate the Queen's Platinum Jubilee in the summer of 2022, the drone display above Buckingham Palace depicted various images, including the face of a corgi. The crowd sighed and chuckled in affection-ate appreciation.

At the Queen's funeral later that year, I am sure I wasn't the only one whose throat tightened and whose eyes pricked with tears when I saw her two Pembroke Welsh corgis, Muick and Sandy, waiting in the quadrangle at Windsor Castle for the cortege to pass.

Their role was a touching tribute to the latest in a long line of dog-loving monarchs.

CHAPTER 6

Training, Scotland

Mary, Queen of Scots, was said to have consoled herself while a child exile in France with the company of more than 20 lap dogs. As she spent most of her adult life imprisoned in various castles, her dogs were her only true friends. When she was executed at Fotheringhay Castle in 1587, her faithful Skye terrier was found quivering under her skirts. It was covered in her blood and refused to leave her side. When it was forced to do so, it refused to eat and died not many days later. The Skye terrier is one of the original breeds of the Hebrides and is described by Dr John Caius in the book I saw in the Kennel Club library.

Famed for their loyalty, the highest profile Skye terrier was Greyfriars Bobby, who visited the grave of his master, John Gray, every day whatever the weather for 14 years. He became a local celebrity and, when the law was changed requiring all dogs to have a licence, the Lord Provost of Edinburgh paid for Bobby to have one. When the dog died in 1872, a granite fountain with a statue was erected in his honour near the Greyfriars churchyard in Edinburgh. The inscription says: 'Let his loyalty and devotion be a lesson to us all.' I've been to see the statue and had to resist rubbing its nose for good luck, because so many people have done so that the top layer has been worn away, leaving it glowing a shade of gold. Well, everyone knows a Skye terrier should have a black nose, so that's just not right.

The Skye terrier is one of around eighteen Scottish breeds. Some of them are obvious because of the name, like the Scottish terrier and the Shetland sheepdog. Others are more subtle, like the Dandie Dinmont, which was named after a character in a Sir Walter Scott novel. Dandie Dinmont was a farmer who owned terriers called Pepper and Mustard from which the breed developed. They are sweet little things with long bodies, short legs, big wide eyes and a fluffy top knot of hair on top of their heads. The Dandie Dinmont is the only breed of dog to have its own tartan, the black and white tartan of Sir Walter Scott.

The king of all Scottish dogs is the deerhound, originally called the Scottish Wolfdog. The deerhound is a larger and thicker-set version of a greyhound with a thick, rough coat. Known as the 'Royal dog of Scotland', it too has a connection with Sir Walter Scott, who described his own deerhound as 'the most perfect creature of Heaven'. Back in the days of the clans, no one below nobleman rank was allowed to own a deerhound and there is no doubt it is a dog that needs space.

They stand at up to 32 inches tall and weigh around 100 pounds (that's just over 7 stone).

Because of their size, deerhounds need particularly good training. Well, to be fair, all dogs need good training, and so I've come to Scotland to discover how to train your dragon. Sorry, your dog.

* * *

I am on the Mainland of Orkney and the wind is howling. I've come here with my lovely producer Karen to record three episodes of *Ramblings*. For the first 15 years, Lucy (the one who didn't like Archie) was pretty much my one and only producer but then she got fed up with the BBC and decided to leave. She says it wasn't me and, as we're still friends now, I think I believe her.

I have a wonderful working life because I get to do lots of different things. There are the high-profile ones like the Olympics or Wimbledon or the Coronation, but whenever I'm asked which is my favourite programme, I don't even have to think.

My answer is always *Ramblings*.

It's not the most glamorous or the best paid, it's not the most high-profile or the most celebrated, but it's the one that is most 'me'. There is no great entourage or production crew, it's just me and my producer carrying a microphone, walking through the countryside as I interview people. It's a walking programme on the radio. If you're reading this in America, you'll think I'm making it up, but honestly, that's what we do. You can find them on BBC Sounds if you don't believe me.

Ramblings has taken me all over the UK to explore different landscapes and meet interesting people. I reckon we've done nearly 500 walks since 1999, when I first presented it, which at about six miles per walk is over 3,000 miles. That's a lot of steps.

We've discussed friendship, mental health, grief, fitness, history, geography, geology, art, music, wildlife and every other subject under the sun (or the rain, or the snow). People open up when they're walking and I think it's because we're looking at the same view, sharing the same experience and that we have time. It's blissfully simple; there is no script and no rush. Rather than staring awkwardly at each other across a studio, reading from a list of questions, we are all looking outwards, marvelling at the beauty around us.

Karen has a labradoodle called Oscar, who she adores as if he were her child. Maybe even more so. Oscar is a fine beast with a lovely temperament and not bad recall. His hair sheds, which is often the case with labradoodles, even if it is assumed by many that they are hypoallergenic. They are not.

Oscar doesn't come on walks with us, but often the guest will have a dog. Recently, we did a walk along the Thames Path with a wonderful poodle crossbreed called Garlic, who acted as a stress indicator to his owner, Freddie, a little boy with PTSD. The dog could sense when Freddie might be about to suffer a panic attack and could give his adoptive parents a warning signal. Usually it was about 20 minutes in advance, which gave them plenty of time to assuage his fears or remove him from a stressful situation. They have used walking as a way of connecting with their son and helping him overcome a traumatic start in life. They are embarking on a series of long-distance paths. Freddie loves it and helps plan the route. Garlic loves it too.

It's the end of January and daylight on Orkney is precious, so whatever the skies are chucking at us, we've got to get out there. Karen and I pull on our boots and wrap ourselves up against the cold. It's important to have a jacket that doesn't rustle because that's an annoying noise for a listener. The same goes for waterproof trousers. Today I've got the lot: leggings, lined winter trousers, a hooded waterproof jacket from the Winter Paralympics which is the warmest thing I've ever owned, thermal socks, gloves and a tube thing I can pull up over my face – although covering my mouth is not really an option as I'm going to have to speak and – just as importantly – be heard.

For the locals this is merely a breeze, but with an average speed of about 60mph and gusts of around 100mph, you wouldn't want to be walking near the cliff edge, particularly after the waitress at the hotel this morning told me a grim story about one of the many cruises that come to the islands for a tour of the main sights.

'The guide took 'em up on the edge and leant over to take a selfie with a puffin.'

'What happened?' I asked.

She paused for dramatic effect and waved her hand. 'Gone.'

Her voice vibrated off the wood panels of the dining room as she delivered the final judgement. 'He fell to the raging seas below.'

Orcadians have a way of telling a story, and they don't bother sugar-coating a grim ending.

With that chilling vision in my mind, I was happy to stick to low shoreline or inland walking with Steve Jenkinson, an expert in dog training. In fact, he's an expert in human training as well, having studied the psychology of people and their pets for a postgraduate diploma. For nearly 20 years he's been the Kennel Club's access and countryside advisor.

Steve undertakes all sorts of consultancy projects to promote responsible dog ownership and to help landowners and farmers have a positive relationship with those walking with dogs through their fields.

Most people in the Orkney Islands have dogs. It's a wonderful environment for them, as long as they don't mind the wind. We have a hire car and when I go to lock it, I realise I'm being an idiot. The day before I had been laughed at by our guest when I clicked the lock button.

'What's the point?' he said. 'It's not going to go anywhere. I don't even know where my front door key is, let alone bother using it.'

I find Steve with his three-year-old dog Teal, sheltering inside the remaining walls of the Broch of Gurness, one of the many ancient fortified ruins on Orkney, which dates back to between 500 and 200 BC.

Teal is a marmalade and white Nova Scotia duck tolling retriever – a breed that originated in Canada as a gundog for duck hunting. The dogs worked both as a lure for the ducks and as a retriever to bring them back once shot.

She is not very big, not much taller than a spaniel, with a double coat, which helps with her buoyancy, and she has webbed feet to help her swim. Teal is hunting in the ruins for a pair of gloves that Steve has hidden. Her tail is wagging as she sniffs around in search of her prize.

'You can tell she's so keen to work,' Steve says, as Teal finds the gloves in a corner of the fortress. She is energetic and clearly intelligent, with a keen sense of smell. She is thrilled with herself as she drops a stinky grey lump at Steve's feet.

'Keeping dogs stimulated is important for all breeds, particularly in the winter,' he explains. 'They shouldn't just be a surrogate for our own wellbeing, the relationship has to work both ways.'

That means keeping the dog happy. Some breeds, like some children, need more stimulation than others.

Our mini search challenge complete, we head out from the protective walls and the wind hits us, coming hard from the west across the Atlantic Ocean from the land of Teal's ancestors in Canada. Immediately it's obvious why any dog walker needs to be able to issue commands to their dog without relying on shouting. The wind takes our voices and deposits them somewhere in Norway.

Walking south-west onto the kelp-covered beach of Aikerness Bay, Teal gallops on ahead. She is bouncing like a puppy. The water to the right froths with white horses and we can see a grey cloud of hail moving across the bay towards us. The wind has got under Teal's tail and makes her giddy with excitement as she rushes around, nose to the ground.

Steve has a whistle around his neck and a series of hand commands that Teal understands. The whistle is soon called into action. The two key commands are a long blast for 'STOP' and a recall with a series of peeps.

'It's always useful to train your dog to respond to a whistle because often you're in a situation when your voice can't be heard,' Steve explains. 'Also, if a whole family walks a dog, they will often use different words and tones for the same command. If they all use a whistle, the command will be consistent.'

I have a flashback to my father screaming into the wind at various dogs who paid not a bit of notice. Boris the boxer is the worst of the lot as he wilfully ignores any shouting and sits there like a lemon on some rotting carcass that he has found. He may stay there for an hour or two and eventually, when he feels like it, make his way home.

I have given my mother a tracker device so that she knows where to find him, but she prefers to keep him on a lead. This is despite the fact that he is capable of pulling her clean over if he sees something he wants to chase. If only he had been trained to obey a whistle. If only …

Steve is expanding on the benefits of the whistle: 'It's neutral in tone and that can be helpful because it means your dog doesn't hear any panic or stress in your voice, which can make your dog feel anxious as well and therefore not want to come back.'

Now that makes sense, and that's where Dad was going wrong. All that anger and anxiety in his voice. No wonder every dog we've ever had ignored him. He used to shout at me and my brother as kids and we pretty quickly became immune. We probably learned it from the dogs. I think he was a shouter because he worked outside all the time and had to shout commands at riders, like a corporal issuing orders to his troops.

I remember when I was riding out on one of the racehorses and he shouted at me in front of everyone else. I'd committed some criminal offence like not going fast enough on my second canter, or going too fast, or not pulling up smoothly enough, or pulling up too early. There were so many things that it could have been, but I was a teenage girl and I was grumpy so I swore back at him. He didn't hear me, which is probably a good thing. I should have given him a whistle instead.

Steve takes me back to the matter in hand: dogs.

'Your dog wants to come back to you when you're happy, not when it thinks it's going to get a row,' he says. 'All you want to communicate is what you want them to DO, not convey an emotion.'

Steve and I can barely hear each other and have to keep stopping to turn our backs to the wind and protect the microphone. Even though we're talking and trying to describe the scenery for the benefit of the radio audience, Steve never takes his eye off Teal. He puts her on the lead when he spots a group of oystercatchers up ahead so that they are not disturbed from their feeding time.

'I guess I can be a bit fastidious about this because I can't very well be telling other people to put their dogs on a lead because of wildlife if I don't do it myself. Also, it's good for dogs to go on the lead and it not be for a bad reason.'

Steve is also fastidious about picking up poo. It's a job all dog owners have to do at one time or another; you might be forgiven for thinking that out in the wild it's OK to 'stick and flick', leave it to decompose or be taken by the waves, but Steve is a stickler for bagging it up and taking it home.

'It's really important, because who knows who might be coming down here with children or buggies or a mobility scooter?' he says. 'It's not nice for any of them to have to cope with it. We also know now that dog poo can carry diseases that can make cattle abort or cause brain disease in sheep, so even out in a rural area, it's a good idea to pick it up.'

I know I'm not the only one who seethes in fury if I see dog-poo bags left tied to a fence or hanging on a bush as if somehow the Poo Fairy is going to come along and spirit them away.

'Even if you've just got one dog walker leaving a bag of poo it reflects badly on us all,' Steve says. 'It's really important to take them away.'

He is so keen on taking his dog poo with him that he doesn't always remember to get rid of it when he gets home, as illustrated by a story that leaves me feeling a little bit queasy. He tells me that he has a specific pocket in his coat that he puts the bags (filled with poo) into. A few years ago he was working in Dublin and when evening came he noticed a strong smell around him.

'I thought I must have trodden in something,' he says, 'but then I realised it was coming from the poo-bag pocket. I'd forgotten all about a bag I'd put in there the day before. I had been on three flights and in the ranger's car all day with that in my pocket. I can only apologise to anyone who was sitting next to me.'

My mouth drops open in shock. I mean, how can you *not notice* that you've spent 24 hours with a bag of poo in your pocket? Steve is very good at his job and has a lot of sensible suggestions, but my God, I am not following his example of having a 'poo-bag pocket' in any jacket, *ever*. He does not share my horror. In fact, he's proud.

'I'd much rather have been smelly than have left it behind.' He laughs. 'That's my badge of honour!'

As a final thought on the dog-poo-bag conundrum, Steve says that 'compostable' is the key word rather than 'bio-degradable'. Compostable bags tend to be made from corn starch and therefore will decompose whether or not they have sunlight. Bio-degradable bags can still be plastic based and need sunlight to break down, which means it's not good if they get buried underground or are in a bin.

Living as remotely as he does, both Steve and Teal need to be good travellers, whether by sea, air or road. Work will generally take him south and Teal often accompanies him to London if he is working at the Kennel Club offices. Teal copes with it all with no noticeable concern. Flying with dogs is so common when you live on an island that there is barely a flight without one, although Teal always travels on the ferry by car with Steve, and it's common to see dogs on the ferries. Most of the small airlines have a special cage for the dog so that it can travel with its owner and see them throughout.

'Dogs are so adaptable,' he says. 'They're brilliant as long as they have good experiences. You have to make sure your dog is not only ever going in the car when they go to the vet, otherwise they will associate being in the car with something they don't like.'

It makes perfect sense when you think about it. Taking your dog in the car for a lovely walk somewhere different means that going in the car is a good thing, not a scary experience. The same with getting in a lift or going on a train or coming with you to the office. Make it all a good experience and a dog will be just fine.

Similar to Sara, the trainer we met at Dogs for Good, everything Steve does with Teal is based on positive reinforcement. He believes in building a good relationship so that your dog wants to do the right thing for you, not because they're scared of doing the wrong thing.

'It doesn't need to always be treats that you're giving them,' he clarifies. 'It can be a ball or a pat or something else they enjoy. In the old days, there was a lot of yanking on the lead and telling off, which was all about control and punishment. Largely we've learnt from the training of guide dogs and assistance dogs that if they're doing things that make them feel good, positive training can work really well.'

Teal is let off the lead again and runs to sniff a mound of kelp. We discuss the behaviour of people as well as their pets; those guidelines of positive reinforcement rather than negative denial can equally work wonders with humans.

Through Steve's professional work, he has experience of all sorts of businesses around the UK that deal with dogs and he advises on how to make the relationship between dog owners and non-dog owners better.

The UK's holiday hotspots get a huge boost from welcoming dog owners, but sometimes all you find as a dog owner are signs saying No Dogs. There used to be pamphlets in Cornwall, for example, with lists of all the beaches on which you couldn't take dogs. Now, there are lists of all the dog-*friendly* beaches. It's a subtle change but it makes a huge difference to how the dog-owning community responds and whether they feel welcomed.

Local coffee shop owners love dog owners because they know they will get a constant stream of customers, whatever the weather. Shops and restaurants can be less keen, but the UK is generally good for dog tourists.

Steve has advised plenty of local authorities on how to improve their relationships with dog owners and how to maximise the benefits they can bring. He strongly believes in collaboration: working with the community of dog owners and dog walkers, rather than imposing decisions or rules on them from afar.

'Dog owners are most influenced by what other dog owners do, so it's important to find out what works for them,' he says. 'They are most likely to take their holidays in the UK rather than go abroad, they are passionate about the outdoors and they love walking.'

It's clear that dog owners are a hugely valuable customer base for UK tourism, so it's a good idea for local authorities to find solutions for them, but we all have to make sure that we keep our dogs under control.

Steve and I discuss footpaths that cross farmland and what to do if you find yourself in a field of cows. Every year between four and six people in the UK are killed because of cattle, and many more injured.

'It tends to be cows with calves, rather than bulls,' Steve says. 'Generally the signs will say "keep your dog on a lead", but quite often the dog will be the focus for the cow and I've known cases where people have been trampled because they kept their dog on the lead.'

So what should we do?

'My advice would be to release your dog if you are threatened by cattle,' he says. 'The dog will be able to run clear and you need to get yourself safely out of that situation.'

Some farmers are making good use of social media or local WhatsApp groups to keep dog walkers informed of where their cattle are, so that they can be avoided.

The only time I've been caught with Archie in a field with cattle was in Cornwall. We were staying on the south coast at Coverack in a gorgeous house owned by some friends of ours. We wanted to explore the local area, so I found a circular walk that happened to include the ice cream parlour at Roskilly's Farm. We all need a goal.

All was going well until we came to a field full of cows. Archie had many faults but his recall was good so I suggested that Alice cross the field first and when she got to the other side, she should call him. I would let him off the lead so he could get across as fast as possible and then I would follow behind him. All very sensible, all very safe, and it worked perfectly – but according to the signs, it was not the done thing.

Steve says this is where we need to have intelligent conversations that encourage walkers to use their initiative. For example, if the footpath goes across the middle of the field but that's where the cattle are gathered, then it is safer to go around the edge or vice versa. The point is to avoid any confrontation between livestock and walkers that might cause injury or damage to either. Keeping your dog under control so it doesn't worry livestock is essential, which brings us back to basic training. Basic recall is not a bonus, it's a *necessity*.

Dog training has evolved over the centuries towards positive reinforcement. As a child of the 1970s and 80s, I clearly remember Barbara Woodhouse on television. I found her rather terrifying, but I would obediently SI-I-T when she appeared and concentrate on her advice. She had a weekly programme called *Training Dogs: The Woodhouse Way* and everything about it was fabulous. A female presenter who was not in any way an object of fashion and who had genuine expertise, plus dogs everywhere. It was appointment viewing.

'There is no such thing as a bad dog,' Woodhouse said. 'It is simply an inexperienced owner.'

Such was Woodhouse's fame that she even got an invitation to America to do a show called *Barbara Woodhouse Goes to Beverly Hills*.

Although she advocated patience, kindness and consistency of tone, she did also use various methods that would not be acceptable today, like a choke chain, which in the wrong hands can cause serious harm. In the UK, Victoria Stillwell would be considered the natural successor to Barbara Woodhouse and she employs a similarly no-nonsense approach with humans. Internationally, the most famous dog trainer is Cesar Millan, who has styled himself as a dog whisperer and has a hugely successful live tour which features dog training lectures and demonstrations. He has hosted multiple TV series and written best-selling books but also seems to have been the subject of multiple lawsuits and plenty of criticism. The world of the celebrity dog trainer is fraught with danger.

Meanwhile in the outer reaches of the Orkney Islands I am enjoying heaven on earth for dogs. There are loads of different walks, dog-friendly cottages, hotels and pubs, and the ferry company providing transport from John O'Groats provides free passage for dogs (in fact, accompanied dogs travel for free on all of Orkey's ferries). The relationship between dogs and people has been part of island life for ever.

In fact, one of the ancient burial tombs proves that dogs have played a key role in the lives of the islanders for thousands of years.

The chambered cairn on Cuween Hill on Mainland Orkney is a burial tomb known as the 'the Tomb of the Dogs'. The information board tells me that the cairn was raised about 5,000–5,200 years ago and that both canine and human bones were found within the tomb.

I get on my hands and knees to crawl inside (not easy with creaking joints and stiff limbs). Raising myself inelegantly to my feet, I stand inside the central room; Karen, Steve and Teal join me and there's room for the four of us. Only Teal can make it into the four smaller side chambers. She takes the opportunity and is busy sniffing around.

It is a beautiful structure that has been built in honour of the whole family, and that includes the dogs. Twenty-four dog skulls were found inside Cuween, along with the remains of eight people. That's a lot of dogs.

The information board tells me that dogs were kept and trained by farmers in Neolithic times as pets, guards and herders of sheep. There is an image by a forensic artist that has been reconstructed from the skull found in the tomb. It is of a long-nosed, short-eared hound that looks a bit like a cross between a lurcher and a border collie.

Despite their wolfy features, these were not wild dogs. They did a job, they were trained and they were part of everyday life. Imagining those ancient people working the land and coping with the elements, I can see them gathered in the evenings with dogs around them, work done for the day, enjoying their company and warmth.

Dogs are good for us and they have been an indispensable part of rural life for ever. Even the Neolithic islanders would have appreciated the joy they bring, and I suspect those dogs would have run up and down the beach as Teal does, wagging their tails as enthusiastically as her.

'The thing I love about dogs is that they live in the moment.' Steve is smiling as he watches Teal running to the water's edge. She puts her nose down briefly and then turns to scamper back to him. 'There's this optimism about them, and whatever happened yesterday, they think today will be good.'

It's a good attitude to have, and for the person in that relationship, the walk with a dog is a chance to clear the mind and focus not on yourself but on your dog.

'Any walk is really good for you,' Steve says, 'but seeing it through the eyes of a dog it is so refreshing.'

That is a good adjective for our day. The wind, the company, the presence of a well-trained dog – it's all so refreshing.

CHAPTER 7

Going to Dog School

Here is a quiz question for you:

How many dog day care centres are there in the UK?
  A. 5–10,000
  B. 20–30,000
  C. 50–60,000
  D. 100–150,000

I love a quiz. I have never been tempted by reality TV, but I am a sucker for a quiz. Ask me to do *The Chase*, *The Weakest Link*, *House of Games*, *Lingo*, *Only Connect* or *Pointless* and I'm in. Christmas a few years ago was ruined by me getting a literature question wrong on *Who Wants to Be a Millionaire* and crashing back to £1,000.

It took me a year to get over it and required a win on *Tipping Point* for full healing. I managed to earn £20,000 for a charity called StreetVet, which provides veterinary care for the dogs of people experiencing homelessness. That made me feel much better.

Anyway, a quick search on the Companies House website reveals that the answer to the question above is D. Well over 100,000 centres across the UK are registered as dog day care companies.

With the huge expansion in dog ownership, the need has grown for places where dogs can be stimulated, fed, cared for and looked after if their owners have to be at work.

Personally, I wish more offices were dog friendly, as I think it would fundamentally change the way we work and would be hugely beneficial to the mental health of those who have to go to an office every day. I realise that's not always practical and therefore dog owners spend a proportion of their salary on making sure their dog is having a better day than they are.

There are luxury dog hotels with room service and a spa, or smaller, more personal services where someone will look after your dog in their own home. If your dog is happy to be around lots of other dogs and would benefit from spending all day playing with mates and running around, there are loads of doggy day care centres that offer a fun, safe environment with full-time staff to keep an eye on all the dogs.

These places sometimes offer an overnight service, but generally speaking, they are the equivalent of kindergarten rather than kennels.

To see for ourselves what it involves, Alice and I have come to Sonning Common just outside Reading in Berkshire to visit Charlie's Place. It's run by Toni Ilsley, who set it up to commemorate her son Charlie.

Charlie always loved dogs and wanted to work with them. Tragically, that dream could not be fulfilled.

'Charlie was diagnosed with a brain tumour in 2015,' Toni says. 'He always wanted a dog from the minute he could speak. I used to work in medicine and we were too busy, so we got this giant house rabbit that we thought would do, but he still wanted a dog.'

Charlie was only eight years old when he started vomiting persistently and had violent headaches. Toni took him to a doctor who at first thought it was a virus but eventually discovered medulloblastoma, a tumour on the brain. He had surgery to remove the tumour, followed by radiotherapy, chemotherapy and stem cell treatment.

'When he got cancer, of course we wanted to get him anything he wanted, so we found Eric.' Toni points down to a little Lhasa apso with a cheeky face.

'Charlie was clear for two years and then it came back.'

It looked as if Charlie had made a remarkable recovery, but in March 2018, two tumours were found on his spine. With no treatment available on the NHS, Toni and her husband Mark raised tens of thousands of pounds to take him to Turkey for revolutionary CyberKnife radiation treatment. They also got Ernie, who is a toy poodle/bichon frise-cross.

Charlie adored Eric and Ernie and was thrilled that he had finally been allowed to have dogs of his own.

'We flew everywhere trying to cure him, and when we were in Mexico staying at this ranch, their dog had had fifteen puppies.' Toni is speaking rapidly and we stroke dogs as we listen to the painful memories. 'Charlie had lost the use of his legs by then and he was in a wheelchair, but he was sat there with puppies all over him and he said, "This is what I want to do when I get older." He was always worried about what he was going to do when he grew up. That was on the Wednesday. He died on Saturday. He was only thirteen.'

There is nothing we can say to comfort her. Nothing we can do to bring him back. So we do what she does, shift our focus to the dogs.

As a way of coping with her grief, Toni threw herself into the one thing she knew Charlie would have loved. She set up at home to start with, but within two months the demand was so high for dog care that she had to expand the business. She went on courses to make sure she qualified for her Level 4 Advanced Canine Behaviour Diploma and researched all the rules to make sure that she was doing it correctly.

We have arrived at 4pm on a damp day. It has just stopped raining and the roads are dotted with puddles. It's pick-up time for a lot of the dogs and I anticipate a scene like the opening sequence of *Love Actually* where everyone at airport arrivals is rushing towards each other with open arms.

'To be honest, it's not like that at all,' Toni tells us. 'They've had such a good time here with all their friends, most of the dogs don't want to go home!'

Toni takes in 30 dogs a day and charges £27 to look after them from eight in the morning until six in the evening. They are fed and all have a bath and a brush before they are collected.

'Are you sure you want to go in wearing those?' Toni asks, looking at our trousers and clean trainers. Her assistant, Emily, laughs and I wonder why.

I notice that Toni, Emily and various other helpers are wearing waterproof over-trousers and wellies. We follow Toni into a large fenced area with about 15 dogs who all come over to say hello and jump up at us. The noise is deafening – high-pitched yapping, low barks and a lot of squeaking – but after a few minutes the cacophony subsides as they realise we are not here to disrupt, just to observe. Our trousers, jackets and shoes are immediately covered in mud, but honestly, it's the friendliest, warmest, kindest mud shower I've ever experienced.

We are surrounded by dogs of all shapes and sizes, all oozing happiness. They've had the best day of their lives and – in true dog style – they can't help but show their joy. We look around and Alice immediately notices something.

'There's no poo anywhere,' she whispers.

I hadn't been on high poo alert but, ever risk-assessing, she has scanned the enclosure for danger.

'We pick it up all day,' Toni explains. 'We've always got two bags on us and you just have to keep on top of it. We spend all day cleaning with disinfectant and hosing things off.'

There is a shed in the corner, an assault course, a slide which apparently the dogs go down of their own accord, a separate enclosure in case a dog needs a bit of quiet time, garden furniture that has been well worn by its canine incumbents, ropes and hosepipes hanging off the branches of trees that can be tugged at any time and a collection of cones that may or may not have been 'appropriated' from local roadworks. They are the favoured peeing spots for the boys.

Toni's husband, Mark, helped clear out the space, which was an overgrown wilderness by some barns. The surface is gravel, which Toni tells me is the outcome of various trial-and-error schemes. Grass is impractical because it turns into a mud bath, and they tried bark but some of the dogs tried to eat it and it got so wet it turned to mulch.

'This has been the best solution so far,' Toni explains. 'The stones are big enough that they don't cause any cuts and the rain runs through it to drain away. They seem to like it and that's the main thing.'

It's like a forest school, and as Toni starts talking about the dogs, she sounds like a teacher who knows each of her pupils intimately.

'They all make friends, and sitting watching them, it's so funny because they all form little gangs. Look at little Arlo – he doesn't want Wallace to go home because they're friends.'

Staffie-cross Keith is a 'lovely dog'. Monty is a beagle/spaniel-cross who can be naughty and that morning came straight in and ate the flowers. Reg is a sausage dog who likes to get himself on to a high surface like a table or a tree stump so he can feel tall. Luna eats a lot of wood so they're always keeping an eye out. The list goes on and on.

Toni has learned the art of patient observation. Rosie was a problem when she first arrived because no one could get her lead off without getting bitten. They bought a plastic hand, so that she would get used to the idea without causing an injury. After three days, she was transformed.

Toni employs students from Berkshire College of Agriculture and offers opportunities to students from The Henley College with learning difficulties. She also has a little boy with cerebral palsy who comes twice a week. He absolutely loves it and the dogs love him and it is clear this is a place that isn't just helping dogs.

Emily tells me about the benefits Charlie's Place has brought to her life. She came on a work placement and then started working full time when she was 17. As well as dealing with bookings and dog care, she helps Toni with the technical side of things, taking videos and photos for the owners.

'I thought I was horrible with people when I first came because I was anxious, but now I talk all day long and Toni says I'm much better.' Emily is smiling. 'I'm so lucky that I got work placement here and that Toni has kept me on. It's such a lovely place to work and I've learned so much. You have to know all about safety and that sometimes the best thing you can do is put a muzzle on a dog so that it can mix safely with the pack. It's not an unkind thing to do, it's the best way to make sure they can all have a good time.'

Emily is overwhelmed by enthusiasm and her love of dogs shines through. There is no doubt in her mind that this is what she wants to do for the rest of her working life. Toni is going to help her do a behaviour course so she has more qualifications. She has found her happy place.

Most of what Toni has learned about dogs has come from observation of pack behaviour for hours and hours every day.

'You always get very low rankers, middle rankers and a couple of high rankers, and those are the ones that can give you trouble if you have two of them. On Fridays we have a problem because Harvey thinks he's higher ranking than Norman and he won't let him play, so he shuts him down. He just won't let Norman play and that puts him in a really bad mood.'

Alice is hugely impressed by the professionalism of Charlie's Place, but, as is her nature, she wants to know about the things that go wrong.

'If someone comes with a problem dog, how do you manage that?' she asks.

Toni is holding Ernie in her arms as she answers.

'People might come and say "my dog's vicious, he's terrible with other dogs", but the dog will come in and be fine. Usually, it's a separation anxiety issue that means they can't stay here. It's particularly common with lockdown dogs.'

She has advised owners to have their dog neutered if it is aggressive and will put on a muzzle if there is any chance of danger to humans or other dogs.

'How many times have you been bitten?' Alice follows up.

Remember, she used to read the news on the *Today* programme. She's seen John Humphrys in action.

'Seriously bitten?' Toni clarifies. 'Only once, by a Staffie. But to be fair, it wasn't her fault. Sometimes when they get excited it can turn into aggression and it's like red mist. She bit through my little finger and my thumb and my ligament was showing. As I say, it wasn't really her fault, but we don't have her any more.'

We are relieved. It's one thing to forgive bad behaviour but it's quite another to put your limbs at risk.

As well as the large outdoor pen, there is a barn that has been transformed into a five-star apartment for dogs. There are different rooms with walls high enough not to be jumpable but low enough to keep the spacious feel, plus a small area where a puppy could go for a rest when life all gets too much. There are sofas, chairs and dog beds, and most importantly, a huge deep metal bath with a hose attachment. The walls are covered in pictures of the dogs that are regulars at Charlie's Place. There are photos of the dogs in fancy dress and brightly painted walls. A sign on the wall reads: HUSBAND AND DOG MISSING. REWARD FOR DOG.

Toni is very interesting about the dangers of humanising dogs. We often expect things from our dogs that are completely unrealistic. She talks about an owner who dropped her dog off and said, 'Please don't teach him to bark. He doesn't bark.'

'We don't let them be dogs. Now we've got a whole bunch of lockdown dogs with problems and their owners don't understand how to deal with it. They expect me to be able to fix it.'

She will always do her best for the dog but I'm getting a sense from a lot of different sources that we need to do more as a nation to understand what owning a dog entails and to take more responsibility for them.

We are failing our dogs and it doesn't have to be that way. Through programmes like *Crufts* and *Ramblings*, I have tried to showcase the benefits of good training, stimulation, nutrition and exercise, but I'm preaching to the converted.

I need to get that message out to the people who think that a dog is just a good photo opportunity for Instagram or a way to make themselves more interesting on TikTok.

I have recently taken on an ambassador role for Pets at Home and I think that's probably the best chance I have of reaching the broadest audience possible. They're a really progressive company whose in-store teams know a huge amount about animal welfare. I have conversations with them about what we can do to promote the right care and to advise on the best ways of coping with welfare issues. I refuse to give up because we can do so much better.

People like Toni can see that all too clearly, because they are with different dogs every day and know what the owners do right and what they do wrong.

Going to Dog School

Toni never expected Charlie's Place to become so popular, but as a business, it is a huge success story. It pays the rent, it pays for five helpers and it pays Toni a wage. Most importantly for her, it also raises money for 'Team Charlie', the charity they started in Charlie's name to help children with serious illnesses.

'If I hadn't started this, I don't know what would have happened. I always said that after Charlie died, I died as well. I was so close to him. He was my youngest and I did everything for him.'

She pauses and we look at what she has created.

'I suppose I still am,' she says. 'I'm doing this and I know he'd love it.'

This is a dog day care centre with a difference because it's doing more than ensuring that dogs have a better life. It's helping to heal a broken heart.

'This place has done more for me than I could have imagined,' Toni says. 'I love these dogs and when we go away on holiday I miss them all. I am outside all day, I'm busy from the minute I get up in the morning and often they come home with me as well. I've got two coming back tonight. Some days it's really hard work, but I wouldn't swap it for the world. They always make me smile.'

Toni's ethos is to let dogs be dogs. They bark, they play, they get dirty. Let it happen and give them a bath afterwards.

* * *

At the other end of the scale is the pet spa. Your dog won't get dirty there.

There are various options in London, including one that offers a pet pedicure that includes a 'paw soak, nail trim, between pads and paw trim, steam towels to soften paw pads and a gentle paw massage'.

There is a fruity facial, a healing bath, a mud bath and fresh-breath treatment. For a bargain £500, you could treat your dog to the full 'Dogviar Deluxe Spa Day Experience', which includes VIP check-in, massage, facial, pedicure and custom coat styling by an actual dog stylist. Now there's a job I did not know existed.

I am fascinated by the dog-spa menu, and it reminds me of a show on TV in the early 2000s called *Footballers' Wives*, where the more outlandish and extreme the storyline was, the better. This is just the sort of place one of their characters would have taken their dog, and I bet they would have booked in for thalassotherapy, where mud containing minerals, sea mud and seaweed extract is gently massaged into the fur and skin to 'remove waste deep inside the pores'. The session is completed with a towel wrap. I guess that's one way to get your dog muddy.

I am starting to think that whoever designed this website is either a genius or a comedian – perhaps both. I'm sure it's doing good business.

Button has jumped on my keyboard as I'm writing this and has somehow clicked on the cat and kitten spa options, which include a waterless bath using foam shampoo, a nail trim, a between pads and paw trim, an ear cleanse, a custom coat styling and a luxury finishing cologne spritz. I read it all out and Alice says, 'Do they also give them a general anaesthetic?'

Some cats might tolerate all that malarkey, but I can tell you that ours most definitely would not.

Back to the dog menu and there is also the option (at an additional cost) of getting your dog's nails painted. I offer no comment, except to say that if you do this to your dog you are dead to me.

* * *

I often say to Alice that when it all goes wrong for me in my broadcasting life, I'll become a dog walker. She is more supportive of that option than my other dream of being a carpenter.

She laughs at that, which I find quite offensive.

I have qualifications: I did woodwork at school and despite slicing into my hand with a chisel, I made some very nice pieces. There was a three-legged stool which my parents had until about five years ago, when one of the nephews sat on it and it snapped in half. I should have oiled it. I also made a stand for a telephone that screwed into the wall. It was a very basic structure but it worked and Dad had it next to his chair for years. He was very appreciative of my carpentry skills.

That is why I dream of one day – in my dotage – making wooden tables and three-legged stools. I could combine it with dog walking, I suppose. At least that way I'd be getting daily exercise.

I have always assumed that dog owners are fitter and healthier than non-dog owners, but now there is proof. A study by the University of Liverpool in 2019 found that dog owners are *four* times more likely than non-dog owners to meet recommended exercise guidelines, with nine out of ten of them completing at least 150 minutes of exercise a week. Dog owners are also more prone to do extra exercise on top of their dog walks, so will often go for a run or a cycle or a swim as well.

Like doggy day care, dog walking has become a massive industry across the UK. It has evolved from a casual, word-of-mouth occupation for people who liked dogs and wanted to help out their friends, to being a regulated, professional service that provides solo walks, group walks, puppy visits, transportation, grooming and dog-sitting. There are even trade associations: the National Association of Registered Pet Sitters and Dog Walkers. It was founded in 2007 and has more than 700 members who all adhere to its code of conduct. There is also the Professional Dog Walkers Association, set up in 2016 to regulate one of the fastest-growing industries in the UK. There are dog-sitters, dog chaperones and dog hotels springing up all across the country. All of which is to say, should I ever decide to become a dog walker, I certainly won't be short of work.

* * *

The first professional dog walker I met was Ellie Hart. We would see her every day in our local park walking a couple of dogs and it took me a while to realise that she seemed to have different dogs on different days.

Ellie worked in restaurants for 15 years but missed having a dog, so borrowed them from other people to give herself a fix. She soon worked out that a lot of people in London were too busy to walk their pets in the middle of the day. She packed in the restaurant business and started a new life as a dog walker, determined to do it properly.

She took out personal and public liability insurance. She made sure she was obeying the guidelines according to the Control of Dogs Order (1992) and the Animal Welfare Act (2006) which state that all dogs in a public place must wear a collar with the owner's name and address on it and that all dogs should be properly cared for.

'It's a huge responsibility,' she told me. 'You have to know what to do if one of your dogs gets attacked or if one of yours attacks another dog. You have the keys to other people's houses and it's a relationship built on trust and reliability.'

We always knew Ellie as 'The Fairy Dog Mother' and she seemed to glow with the joy of her job. She never took more than four dogs at a time and she did a lot of homework to make sure they all mixed well.

'You have to meet the dogs and understand their personality before you take them out with other dogs,' she told me. 'Just like people, some dogs don't like each other, and you need to take them in groups that get along.'

When Ellie got married, her guest list was made up of more dogs than people.

'We had seventy dogs at our wedding.' She laughs. 'They sat on the pews and they all behaved! We had dog biscuits instead of confetti. I had family there and obviously my husband, but as we left the church he was a bit upset that I was kissing all the dogs rather than him.'

When Alice and I had our civil partnership in 2006, we wanted to take Archie to the ceremony. Sadly, that wasn't allowed, but we had all our photos with him and there is one proudly hanging on the wall. He looks so smart and sort of proud. We do too.

Ellie's job meant that she had a very clear understanding of the demographics of first-time dog ownership and how the families or individuals did not always understand the commitment required. She still simmers with anger about one situation.

'I've had a dog that I have walked every day of its life,' she told me. 'I've had it for Christmas, for summer holidays, to the extent that I wanted to say to them "you might as well get a cushion", because they took no responsibility at all. When I started doing dog walking, people would say "what happens when we go on holiday?" and I wanted to say, "you need to have thought about that before you got this dog".'

Ellie is the sort of person who would have given clear and honest feedback. It may have lost her the odd client, but in her eyes the dogs always come first.

'The amount of people that ask me to walk their dog but say "could you not get him dirty?" Honestly, it's a dog, it's going to get dirty.'

She has now moved out of London with her husband and daughter and is a certified dog behaviourist, but she credits the profession of dog walking for transforming her life.

'It's kept me fit. When I was at the peak of it I was doing five or six walks a day so a huge amount of miles. You can't have a day off sick. You have to crack on with it, which makes you a stronger person. It's very sociable and it really brightens your day – every time you open a door there's a dog delighted to see you. You are the best thing on the planet for those dogs and they don't forget you. Years later, if I come back to this park and blow my whistle, it's like being Tarzan because all the animals come running to me.'

Speaking of our local park and dogs coming running, Alice and I have just been to the café to meet up with our friend Joss and her cockapoo, Betty. There is no dog on earth that shows her love as much as Betty. We have known her since she was a puppy and she has a super-sense that tells her when we are within half a mile. She must know our voices, because out of nowhere, she will appear, hurtling towards us with her tail wagging. Even Archie didn't love us as much as Betty does. She is full on with her affection and her energy.

The cocker spaniel/poodle-cross has rapidly become one of the most popular dogs in the country, but they should come with an energy certificate. Vivacity is their calling card, and although Betty is now 12 years old, she is showing no signs of slowing down.

My go-to expert, Jessica Holm, explains why: 'The poodle is very intelligent, full of beans and needs something to do with its mind, while the cocker spaniel is like a double-A battery. You put those two things together and you get hybrid vigour. I've met so many people who have bought cockapoos because they think it's the perfect size and cuddly like a teddy bear but then they're tearing their hair out because it needs stimulation and exercise all the time.'

There is an assumption that a cockapoo coat will not shed and will be hypoallergenic, but that is not guaranteed. The same with labradoodles. Their coats need a lot of maintenance to prevent matting. They are delightful to look at but they are not an easy option.

Despite all of those caveats, if ever called upon we would adopt Betty in a heartbeat. She is one of the most warm and lovely characters I've ever met. If ever I am feeling anti-social (which doesn't happen often), my mantra is 'be more Betty'.

Alice's mother, Pam, was like Betty in her emotional openness. She was a hugger and a frequent expresser of her love for everyone, and would throw open the front door before Alice had even parked the car outside her parents' house in Esher and run towards her with arms open wide, crying, 'Tiny Wee!'

Going to Dog School

Alice was always small and when she was born (at home in her mother's bedroom) she weighed only five and a half pounds. Hence the nickname. If she were a dog, she'd have definitely been in the Toy group.

When Pam finally had to go into a care home, she made friends with absolutely every resident and carer. She loved everyone and would help feed those who were struggling or give an arm if they needed support, even though she wasn't that steady herself by that stage. The world lost a warm and loving soul when she left us in 2018.

My grandmother, on the other hand, was not like Betty or Pam. Not at all. She was formal, upright and smacked of the British stiff upper lip. One could put it down to her upbringing, I suppose. Her mother died when she was only eight years old and she was brought up by a nanny at her grandparents' vast estate at Knowsley Hall in St Helens. She was home schooled and her only friends were her half-sister Ruth, any young house-keeping staff, the groom and the gardener. Oh, and the dogs.

Although famously prickly with humans (apart from my brother, whom she adored), Grandma would show unfettered affection towards her dogs. I mentioned earlier that she had a very greedy Labrador called Chico. Throughout her life she also had whippets. They had names like Dawn, Dusk and Noon.

Whippets were recognised as a breed by the Kennel Club in 1891 and they were the first in the world to have their own breed club, formed in 1899. They had been around for centuries before then, and small greyhound-like dogs feature in tapestries and artwork from medieval times.

In the UK, they were particularly popular amongst miners in the north-east of England. Bred down from small greyhounds, they were used to course rabbits and it became a popular betting pastime. In an early form of 'drag hunting', the sport was adapted so that the whippets chased a rag that had been soaked in scent down alleyways or straight tracks. That earned them the nickname, 'the lightning-rag dog'.

Whippets have maintained their speed and their love of the chase.

Our friends Chris and Derek followed Sid with various other whippets, often acquired 'pre-loved'. They prefer that term to 'second-hand' and often it's because a whippet has become part of a pack that is too big for its specific needs. Chris and Derek offer a loving and quiet home, free from children and full of comfortable beds, chairs and sofas where the whippets have free range.

Their current dog Mo does not look altogether pure whippet. I pointed this out when I first met him, believing as I do that it's always best to be honest and direct.

'Mo's head is very wide for a whippet, you know. I'm pretty sure there may be a bit of Staffie in there,' I said. I probably should have been a bit more sensitive.

Chris was deeply offended, but Derek shared my suspicion that Mo was not the pure-bred pedigree whippet he had been sold as. It doesn't matter, of course, and he's a lovely dog, but it's always worth knowing what's what, as some breeds have inherent health issues that are not present in others.

They had his DNA checked out, using a service akin to a canine ancestry search for humans. The analysis came back and they opened it nervously. Sure enough, there was not just Staffordshire bull terrier detected as a parent but American bully and American Staffordshire terrier in his grandparents as well. Turns out Mo has more Staffie in him than whippet.

No wonder he's getting a little wide around the girth in his middle age.

The prettiest whippet I've met is Olive, who belongs to Jennifer Saunders. Just before the first Covid lockdown of March 2020, Alice and I met up with Jennifer, the renowned actress, comedian and writer who co-created one of my favourite shows, *French and Saunders*, on Hampstead Heath, a huge public area in north London with woodland, ponds, grassy hills and endless footpaths. It's very easy to find places to walk in London, with 3,000 parks and green spaces to choose from, covering over 35,000 acres.

I've known Jennifer and her comedy partner, Dawn French, for many years, and they are brilliant writers and hilarious, generous women. We have stayed with them both: we took Archie to Devon where he disgraced himself by spreading mud all over Jennifer's very smart (and clean) guest room, and then in Cornwall he decided to take himself on a self-guided tour of Dawn's whole house. Her West Highland terrier was very unimpressed.

This time, Alice and I were taking a slice of Archie's birthday cake (he had turned 15 the weekend before) with us to Hampstead Heath. The cake was not for Jennifer, it was for Olive – it was a special dog-friendly cake that had been given to Archie at Crufts. Olive – an elegant and beautiful blue whippet – has been by Jennifer's side as a constant companion for well over a decade.

'A lot of people said, "oh, whippets are so shivery and scared all the time", but I took her everywhere with me when she was a puppy,' Jennifer said. 'I took her into dressing rooms, into meetings, in the car, and she settles straight away. As long as she's got something to lie on and something to cover her, she's fine.'

Olive came into Jennifer's life in 2010 and she was a much-needed pick-me-up. She adapts to London life when necessary and loves it in Devon, where Jennifer and her husband, Ade Edmondson, have a home.

'We had two border terriers before, who I adored but they were very busy and yappy and used to fight a lot. Ade would have been happy without a dog but I really wanted one. It was after I'd had my breast cancer and I thought "my treat will be to have a dog". She added that they are terribly clean: 'Mud doesn't stick to them somehow.'

In many ways, Olive is perfect. The one downside to her temperament is that, like James Bond, underneath the charming, sleek exterior, she is a trained killer.

'She's not very good with small animals, particularly squirrels,' Jennifer said, as Olive's ears pricked up and her nose twitched. 'I can't walk her safely in Hyde Park, for example, because so many tourists feed the squirrels and she has been known to take one from right under their noses. It doesn't always go down well.'

Picture the scene: American tourists happily walking in Hyde Park snapping photos of each other, suddenly screaming in horror as Olive dives in to catch a grey squirrel and kill it with a swift shake of the head. Then the double take as the actual Jennifer Saunders tries to call her off. As we all know, that is never going to work. Olive is very biddable and bonded, but when 'the squirrel red mist' descends, she ignores everything else. There is no stopping her on her mission.

That's the thing with whippets: they are born and bred to seek, catch and kill. I'm not sure that Eric or Button would appreciate having one in the house. They're a beautiful breed, but not quite the new dog for us.

CHAPTER 8

Good for Our Health

There was a dark and distressing time in British science when dogs were used in laboratory experiments (as were other animals) to test all sorts of substances and medicines. It is no longer legal, thankfully, to test cosmetic products or household products on dogs in the UK but some testing continues, controversially, for medical and veterinary products. In these procedures, dogs are injected or fed with drugs and, then monitored to discover if there are negative side effects. These side effects are things like vomiting, internal bleeding, seizures and organ damage. None of them are comfortable and, not surprisingly, there is a strong and consistent objection to the use of dogs in this role, including from the Kennel Club, who have campaigned in opposition to 'the use of dogs in chemical toxicology and drug safety evaluation conducted primarily for the benefit of humans'.

There are far better and kinder ways in which dogs can help us with medical advancement. For one thing, they can sometimes tell us when we have a disease even quicker than a doctor can.

'I was known as the mad dog lady,' Claire Guest says with a wry smile. We first met a few years ago at Crufts when Claire appeared on the programme to discuss her research and work. We are now talking on a Zoom call. She is co-founder, CEO and chief scientific officer of Medical Detection Dogs, set up in 2008 and based in Milton Keynes, though they work throughout the UK.

Before that, Claire worked at Hearing Dogs for Deaf People and had a deep understanding of assistance dogs and how much they can improve a person's life and outlook. She developed an interest in the medical side of things almost by accident.

She had a friend called Jill who worked with her at Hearing Dogs.

'Jill told me about her Dalmatian,' she says, 'who kept sniffing and licking a mole on her calf and it wouldn't give up, even if she had trousers on. She was in her late teens, early twenties, and couldn't understand what was happening. She went to her GP to have it removed and was told it was malignant melanoma which would have probably been fatal if she hadn't found it so early.'

Years later, Claire heard an interview on Radio 4 with Dr John Church, who was talking about his work in Rwanda and how he had relied on his own sense of smell to help diagnose diseases. She started to think that if a human could smell disease then the superior skills of a dog could be even better at it.

She heard a few other examples that suggested that dogs were very effective at early detection of cancer and decided that she wanted to work on the ability of dogs to detect human disease by scent. Along with Dr Church and Jill, she published the first study in the world in the *British Medical Journal* in 2004 from a small training sample of dogs.

I am no scientist, but I find this fascinating.

When we are ill, our personal smell (which is unique, like our DNA) changes. Metabolic diseases and cancers alter our body cells and when the cells change, they produce volatile organic compounds, known as VOCs.

The VOCs enter the bloodstream and are exhaled in our breath, excreted in urine and sweated out through our skin. We humans can't smell it, but to a dog, we stink. That change in odour can start to happen way before any lumps or moles are visible and much earlier than tremors or seizures might occur.

With noses that have a large surface area and a much higher concentration of olfactory receptors (up to 300 million compared to our 6 million), dogs also have a special part of their nose called the vomeronasal organ which allows them to detect pheromones and other chemical signals that humans can't. They smell on the out breath as well as the in breath, and can take in a whole range of different aromas.

To understand the supremacy of their smelling capacity, Claire puts it this way: 'Humans with a good sense of smell might be able to detect the smell of a teaspoon of sugar in a cup of tea or coffee. Dogs are able to smell a teaspoon of sugar in an area of water the size of two Olympic-sized swimming pools.'

That's why they can smell drugs or explosives and can detect changes in sugar levels to help those with diabetes or the imminent onset of an epileptic seizure. Dogs are smelling all of us in the equivalent of seeing us in ultra-high definition.

The trick is to channel that ability so that they can accurately assess and diagnose a given disease from a large batch of samples. That's where Medical Detection Dogs has made ground-breaking progress.

Claire's own dog Daisy was a specialist in prostate cancer. She sniffed more than 6,500 samples and detected more than 550 cases of prostate cancer. She was awarded the Blue Cross Medal in 2014. Claire was always very proud of Daisy's work, but she has an even greater reason to be grateful to her remarkable fox-red Labrador.

'She had been behaving very oddly around me and it was almost as if she was upset with me. She would look at me with her big brown eyes and I didn't know what it was. I took the dogs for a walk and they all jumped out of the back of the car but Daisy wouldn't move,' she remembers. 'She was staring and although it wasn't as intense as her reaction when detecting prostate cancer, which is what she'd been trained for, she nudged at me. I found a lump that was very deep-seated breast cancer.'

At the time, Claire was too young to have a mammogram, so it would not have been picked up until it was too late.

The consultant she saw was so impressed with the dog's ability to detect such a tiny lump that he became one of the trustees of Medical Detection Dogs.

The first wave of interest in the charity was huge and there was a lot of media coverage as it combined two things that the British love: talking about their health and dogs. Then cynicism set in, especially amongst medical professionals, who assumed there was no scientific rigour to the process.

Daisy's insistence that something was wrong didn't just change Claire's medical history, it also renewed her zeal to spread the word.

'Instead of thinking, "well, if dogs can smell it, let's work with them and see what they can tell us", the medical world was very sceptical,' Claire tells me. 'The fact that Daisy had done this for me made me even bolder and I told our story with even more energy, without being knocked back by the negativity.'

Daisy is sadly no longer around. She died in 2019, and Claire's voice cracks with emotion as she tells me what happened.

'Heartbreakingly, she died of canine breast cancer,' she says. 'That was devastating. She was thirteen and a half, so she was a good age, but it was still such a shock. It was a very aggressive tumour and killed her within a month. I just felt awful that I wasn't able to do for her what she did for me.'

Daisy's work in detecting prostate cancer helped Medical Detection Dogs to their biggest breakthrough. They were approached by The Prostate Cancer Foundation for help in developing an artificial nose, based on the sensitivity of a dog's nose, to discriminate between different smells. With funding from America, where they are rather more open-minded about learning from the natural world, Dr Andreas Mershin has developed a 'robotic nose' that could eventually become an app on a phone. It's extraordinary stuff.

'He is the most amazing man,' Claire says. 'He's incredibly intelligent and loses me in about the first sentence, but he's so passionate and has this huge belief that if you want to make incredible breakthroughs, you need to look at nature. He understands that the sense of smell is hugely complex and it's a perception rather than a lock-and-key outcome. There are loads of things that go into that perception and it's affected by a huge range of things, which is why the detection of diseases through olfaction has been much harder and more complicated than anyone thought because it's not just that one odour. The dog understands that pattern and the subtleties of different smells.'

Knowing that early treatment is essential to recovery, Claire and the team at Medical Detection Dogs have been training dogs to smell Parkinson's disease at its very earliest stages and urinary tract infections, which can cause so many different issues in older people.

All of the dogs that work for Medical Detection Dogs live in homes rather than kennels and have a relatively short working day so that they are not over-stretched.

In the same way that Dogs for Good trains with positive rewards, the dogs are rewarded for detecting a specific odour.

They are also rewarded if they scan a collection of samples and correctly identify that none of them are positive.

For the bio-detection work, gundogs like spaniels, Labradors, golden retrievers and Hungarian vizslas tend to work well because scent detection has been their purpose since they were first developed. They love their work and get a dopamine hit from that challenge so it's relatively easy to transfer that skill to sniffing out disease and being rewarded for it. Medical Detection Dogs has about forty bio-detection dogs and they all have a specific disease for which they are trained.

The charity has also placed over 150 medical assistance dogs, which are the ones helping people with diabetes, epilepsy or narcolepsy. Breeds that bond well with humans are the best ones for assistance dogs, so poodles or poodle-crosses can work really well.

As with Dogs for Good, the basis of any relationship with an assistance dog is good training. They are far more intelligent than we give them credit for but, like a child who will get away with doing less at school if no one is marking their work, a dog can only learn skills if they are taught consistently and clearly. The good news for dog lovers is that scientists have largely moved away from using dogs as testing pin cushions and, in the case of Medical Detection Dogs, are working with them instead of experimenting on them.

Another area of scientific study has confirmed that dogs are good for our mental health. Dog lovers don't need surveys or studies to prove what they already know, but if you want to impress your friends or, like me, you're mugging up for *The Wheel*, the detail is interesting. People with dogs have lower blood pressure and are less likely to develop heart disease. Playing with dogs or petting them elevates oxytocin, and promotes the release of serotonin, prolactin and dopamine, which creates positive feelings.

I have a friend who is brilliant at her job, kind, intelligent and fun to be around, but she suffers from high levels of anxiety. She has started to go to 'puppy yoga' and has found it incredibly helpful. If you're wondering what the hell puppy yoga is, it's the same as yoga but there are puppies around to stroke, play with, laugh with and look at. You don't make the puppies do the exercises with you, although it does bring a whole new meaning to 'downward dog'.

Puppy Yoga UK was founded in Liverpool by students in the final year of a psychology degree who understood the mental health benefits of being around pets. They have since expanded their business to Manchester, Leeds, Birmingham, Newcastle, Sheffield and Nottingham.

The benefit for the puppies is that – provided the classes are carefully planned to take into account their needs to eat, drink and rest regularly – they get to socialise with a number of different people in a calm and controlled situation. The benefit for the humans is that they get to do their yoga while being surrounded by adorable puppies. If I was supple enough to even consider yoga as something better than torture, I'd sign up right now.

In the USA and here in the UK, dogs are proving a valuable asset in the treatment of post-traumatic stress disorder (PTSD). Service Dogs UK is a charity that works with people who have served in the armed forces and it draws on the associated benefits of walking a dog as well as the specific tasks a dog can perform. Having a dog means that even the most isolated or anti-social person has to go out, and they have a chance to interact with other dog owners in as little or great a depth as is comfortable.

The feedback from veterans suggests that having a dog has helped them cope with emotional numbness (a symptom of PTSD), connect with other human beings, given them purpose, independence and a sense of pride, and made them smile again. That in itself is a pretty powerful cocktail of positive treatment, but let's add to the mix the well-trained dog's ability to wake someone up if they're having a nightmare, comfort them if they're having a panic attack, bring them back into the present situation if they're suffering from disassociation or remind them to take their medication.

All in all, you have a living, breathing, walking, barking miracle. Having a dog may not be the panacea for every illness, but I reckon they can help solve a lot of the problems of the modern world and that we can learn a lot from them.

The training at Medical Detection Dogs was key in the emergence of a real-life pet detective. Former police officer Colin Butcher had the idea to set up a service finding missing pets and founded The UK Pet Detectives in 2005. He initially focused on missing horses and dogs before realising that most of the calls he got came from cat owners.

He needed to find a dog that didn't want to chase cats but could find them. He came across Molly, a cocker spaniel who had proved too much for her previous owners. Colin knew immediately that she could be the right dog for the task.

'I've been around hundreds of dogs and have never seen one that has her focus,' he said. 'She's so good at what she does and will just keep going and going.'

He took Molly to the Medical Detection Dogs centre in Milton Keynes to learn how to channel her scenting skills and she learned 'scent matching' so that if she is given a hair sample from a certain cat, she will track it and ignore other cat smells. When she finds the missing pet, she lies down so the cat isn't scared into running off and Colin can approach calmly and quietly. They receive around fifteen calls a week from people needing help to track down a missing pet and Molly is always keen to help.

Cats often go missing of their own accord, and in most cases they will make their way home again, but there is always the fear that a missing dog may have been taken deliberately. I was asked to present a series in the summer of 2023 called *Lost Dogs Live*, as part of a dog-safety campaign launched by Channel 5.

Figures suggest that around 2,000 dogs are stolen in the UK every year. That's five dogs every day. Sometimes they are held to ransom, but often they are sold on within days and the original owner never finds them again. It is a hugely traumatic situation for both the dogs and the human beings.

The UK Government published a Pet Theft Taskforce report in September 2021, which recommended changes to the existing law so that dogs are recognised as sentient beings rather than property. The change in status was passed into law with the Animal Welfare (Sentience) Act (2022) and it will mean much tougher sentences for those who are found guilty of stealing dogs.

There is still, obviously, the challenge of finding the perpetrators and of preventing the criminals from taking dogs in the first place. Technology can help and tracker tags are getting smaller all the time so can now be worn easily on a collar or harness without feeling like a lump of lead. They are excellent for finding dogs that go roaming and get lost, but of course thieves will remove a collar straight away, so they can't always help find stolen dogs. Microchips are essential in identification for dogs that are found and they have helped reunite many a separated family, even after months or years.

There is also a far-reaching network of dog owners looking out for dogs that have been reported missing. This is one area where social media can be hugely helpful, so if your dog gets lost or you fear it has been stolen, use it all. There is a big Facebook group run by DogLost.co.uk, where owners of missing dogs can spread the message and a photo far and wide so that people are on the lookout.

I'd also get the technology experts on the case. For example, the Ayrshire Drone Dog Rescue team, who use drones to search for missing dogs. They can cover a huge area and use thermal imaging to pick up the warmth of a dog even if it is hiding out of sight. They managed to rescue a tiny Pomeranian called Aurora who had run off and disappeared for four days after being scared by a large dog barking at her. The drone tracked her and then backed off for fear of scaring her even more. The volunteers from the rescue team laid a trail of sardine spray for half a mile to gently coax her into a cage and back to the safety of her home.

Drones have also been used in rescue situations when dogs have ended up in inaccessible areas or on islands with the tide coming in. If it is unsafe for a human to try to venture out, a drone with a sausage dangling from a line is the answer.

Beauty's Legacy is a charity that helps investigate cases of dog abduction and activates thousands of people to help with the search. Lisa Dean, its founder, offers 24-hour support for the families affected and it doesn't stop if the dog is successfully found and returned. She has worked on hundreds of cases and knows that dogs can be badly affected by the experience and need a lot of aftercare to overcome the trauma.

If ever you need a pick-me-up, search online for dogs being reunited with their owners. Some have been apart for months, even years, but once the dog smells the scent of its human, the reaction is overwhelming. Language can't do justice to the emotion expressed in a dog wagging every part of its body as it reconnects with the person it loves.

Sentient beings? A million times YES.

CHAPTER 9

Puppies, Worcestershire

As I mentioned, I love a quiz show, so when I was asked to appear on *The Wheel* for a fourth time, I leaped at the chance. The series is filmed in the middle of an airfield in Hertfordshire where they've built a massive studio. There is a giant circular structure with big chairs that we, the so-called experts, are locked into so we can't fall out as the wheel spins round. It's a concept devised by Michael McIntyre and I love the way he presents it with so much energy and humour.

I chose dogs as my specialist subject and during the course of my homework, I mugged up on all sorts of things. For example, did you know that the most successful breed of dog at Crufts is the cocker spaniel? It didn't come up as a question, but I feel compelled to share it here. The English cocker spaniel has won Best in Show seven times and the American cocker spaniel once.

Spaniels are one of the oldest breeds of dog in the world and feature in Chaucer's *The Canterbury Tales* and Shakespeare's plays. They have literary heft.

It is thought that their name derives from *chiens de l'Espagnol,* or from Hispania as they originated in Spain. Like a lot of breeds, they were separated according to size, and eventually the smaller ones became cocker spaniels and the larger ones springer spaniels. Nowadays there are as many types of spaniel as flavours of ice cream: springer, cocker, clumber, Sussex, field, cavalier King Charles, Tibetan and Welsh.

They are also related to setters and share that lovely long, soft coat as well as a friendly and outgoing personality. My headmistress at school, Miss Farr, had Irish setters and they were beautiful beasts. She used to walk them through the woods in the mornings and until recently she was breeding them in Herefordshire. In fact, she emailed me after Crufts to tell me that the winner of the Best of Breed in the Irish setters was closely related to her favourite dog, Darcey. Dog breeders and teachers have a lot in common – they never forget.

Setters are elegant and slightly dippy. I like them but they're a big dog and you need a lot of space. I think we need to set our sights a little smaller.

My Aunt Gail (Dad's younger sister) has always had English springer spaniels. She lives in America, which makes it a bit tricky to dogsit for her, but whenever we've met her dogs, we've loved them. Alice had a particular soft spot for Bunker, who was very cuddly.

Aunt Gail has always followed a golf theme for her dogs' names. Along with Bunker, she has had Birdie, Divot, Mulligan, Wedge and Putter.

Currently, she has Rory, named after Rory McIlroy, and most recently Kizzie, who is apparently named after Kevin Kisner. You may not have heard of Kevin Kisner and you would not be alone. He is not exactly high profile on this side of the pond. I'd have gone for Jordan or Scottie or Tiger. I mean, they've all won Majors and everyone knows who they are.

There is also the fact that Kizzie is a girl, so you'd have thought maybe one of our female stars like Charley Hull or Georgia Hall might have given inspiration. Aunt Gail likes to promote her British roots and this was the perfect opportunity.

However, Kevin Kisner the man comes from Aiken, the small town in South Carolina where Aunt Gail and her dogs live, so she wanted to honour him. I don't know how he feels about having his name shouted around his home town, but as she'll probably give a copy of this book to his mother, I'd better retract all that and say that Kizzie is the best name she's ever chosen. Even for a bitch.

Aunt Gail looks a little like Julie Walters and I often think of her famously hapless depiction of Mrs Overall when I see her walking her dogs in Aiken's Hitchcock Woods. She carries a small spade and runs after her dogs to flick anything they may leave on the path into the undergrowth where no one will tread on it. Aunt Gail is quite enthusiastic in her flicking, and if you're behind her, you need to be on your guard because she is not always that accurate. I haven't told her about Steve Jenkinson's rule that dog poo must always be picked up and taken away. I know she would constantly forget to empty her pockets and I'm not sure I can do that to her family.

Walking the dogs with Aunt Gail is a dangerous business but it's also great fun because the woods are vast and the dogs enjoy themselves so much. They do not always come back when they are called, but that's part of the jeopardy – along with flying poo. She loves her springer spaniels because she says they're 'incredibly loyal, sweet and smart'.

She means the latter in the more common American sense of clever. Not in the traditional English sense of well-dressed. At least, I assume so.

A springer spaniel would be a lovely new dog for us, I think, but first we are going to check out their smaller cousins; Alice and I are going to see cocker spaniel puppies.

I know, this could be dangerous.

My aforementioned *Ramblings* producer, Karen, has a sister-in-law who is one of the top cocker spaniel breeders in the country. She has had outstanding success at Crufts and is hugely respected for breeding dogs who not only look the part but have a lovely temperament.

Breeding, of course, means mating. Now, we need to talk about mating. If you are at all prudish, skip ahead because what follows may be graphic in detail but it's essential knowledge, especially if you are going to try and breed a showdog.

My father's lurcher Bertie was a fine stud dog, much in demand in the local area and regularly employed. Mum and Dad had a few litters of their own, with Cindy the willing mother, but I clearly remember walking in on the mating ritual by mistake, to see the two dogs back to back like the pushmi-pullyu animal in *Dr Dolittle*. They were connected but facing in opposite directions. It was horrifying.

I asked my dad what was going on. 'Don't worry, they're tied,' he said.

I had no idea what this meant and, given my trauma, have never dared revisit the image. Until now.

Jessica Holm is my guru in all such matters, and I knew she could talk this through with the precision and sensible tone of a biology teacher, so I rang her. As an opener to a conversation it was, I grant you, unusual:

'What actually happens when two dogs mate?'

She laughed. I told her about the weird vision of Cindy and Bertie being back to back and she said, 'Ah yes, they were tied.'

'Yes, that's what my father said. But I don't know what that means.'

* * *

So Jessica gave me a biology lesson. A dog's penis has a bone in it called a baculum. It is quite a long thing, because it's got to get a long way in, and at the base of it is the bulbis glandis, which swells when the dog ejaculates. Ideally, the whole bulbis needs to be inside the bitch, and she then tightens her vaginal muscles, which holds the dog in place.

The sperm comes in fractions, with lubricant first, then sperm, then more lubricant. When a dog is tied with a bitch, he will then turn himself, because it's more comfortable for him to be standing on all four legs. I still don't quite understand how the dog achieves that when his penis is pointing in the other direction. It's like an extreme *Kama Sutra* position that looks horribly painful, but apparently is not.

The tie is entirely governed by the bitch. She will hold him for as long as necessary and when she finally relaxes the muscle, that will release him.

Whenever she breeds her own dogs, Jessica makes sure she stays in the room.

'You should never be invasive,' she explains, 'but calm, kind and gentle. The longest tie I've sat through was two and a half hours. My knees were wrecked.'

Usually, she adds, it takes between 20 and 40 minutes.

The reason Jessica stays in the room is not out of curiosity. It's because things can go wrong.

'I had a dog once who would faint as he ejaculated because there was so much blood flooding to the area,' she explains, adding that often the bitch may be in pain if it's her first time. 'You have to be there to make sure she doesn't try and get rid of him while they are tied. You should stay with them to protect both dog and bitch.'

I'm not sure I could take the responsibility.

I ask Jessica about creating the right atmosphere for a loving relationship. Do you need to light candles, put roses in a vase, play soft music? Again, she laughs and then she tells me about Marvin, her friendly French bulldog.

'If the dog knows what he's doing, it can happen in a garage. It doesn't matter. Marvin is an incredibly good stud dog. You show him a bitch in season and, as long as she's on her right day, he will do what he needs to do.' Within minutes, she says, he's asking to play with his toys again.

The problems come when you're using pets – dogs that have not been trained in the art of breeding, as Jessica explains.

'There was a dog I bred and sold as a pet, and I saw him again as a two- or three-year-old and loved him, so I asked if I could borrow him for my bitch.'

You see, this is the sort of conversation dog breeders have with each other. Not how are you and isn't the weather hot for this time of year but, your dog looks better than I'd imagined. Can I borrow him to have sex with my bitch?

So, this poor dog arrives at Jessica's house to be greeted by a bitch mad in season and he doesn't know what he is meant to do. He thought he was just coming for a short break at a B&B.

'He didn't have a clue and cared even less,' Jessica says. 'The bitch was literally sitting on his face, running around and presenting herself, but he didn't know what he was doing. We went on like this for three days, but finally I managed to persuade him that it would be a good idea to mount her. He inserted himself into her for about ten seconds, there was no tie, no nothing, and he wouldn't even think of doing it again. I wrote it off as being a useless mating but, surprise, surprise, we got a litter of eight puppies.'

Well, there we are, a happy ending with no need for the painful bottom-to-bottom manoeuvre. I'd say that's a very sensible dog. Jessica seems to read my mind and makes it clear that it is not a winning approach. No, Marvin is the champion in that department. He's enthusiastic and efficient. 'He's like a little sex machine, clever boy,' she says, with real pride.

As well as finding a dog who can actually do the deed, he needs to be the right choice for your bitch. Just like mating racehorses, you're looking for strengths in one side of the pedigree that can balance out weaknesses in the other. Jessica says you have to be honest about your bitch's plus points and her faults. So, she may have a wonderful head but her ribcage could be better or her coat smoother or fuller. Then you look for a dog who is strong in those departments. That, she explains, used to be the purpose of dog shows. You could find something you like that has the qualities maybe your dog is missing. Then you check the pedigree to see if the families align.

'So you're thinking about breed standard,' Jessica explains, 'and how to improve your line. Then there's pheno-type and genotype.'

She's lost me again, so I ask for an explanation. Pheno-type, she explains, is the dog's physical appearance, where genotype is its genetic make-up. It's very important to find out as much as possible about genotype in particular.

'Knowing pedigrees is so important,' says Jessica, 'because when you know generations of a family, you understand not just the look but the behaviour of certain lines. Grandparents can be on both sides, so long as you know they were healthy. The danger comes in some modern dog breeding, where it can be so much more about phenotype, where dogs are being produced for a certain look, to suit a fashion. If you concentrate on that, you will create problems. Selection is based on knowing what you need and knowing what you want.'

With all that in mind, I am ready to visit an active breeder of cocker spaniels. Karen has heard that her sister-in-law has a litter of puppies that have not yet left home and that's enough to persuade us to set off to Worcestershire.

Talking of not leaving home, Pat Whitehead hasn't been away overnight since 2019. She has only had three holidays in thirteen years and all of them involved either judging dog shows, going to dog shows or meeting other cocker spaniel breeders.

I am not exaggerating when I say that her dogs are her life. She worked for Marks & Spencer for 25 years but as soon as she could retire, she devoted herself to dog showing. She breeds a couple of litters a year to pay for the costs of travelling to the shows and for the upkeep of her dogs. She doesn't breed for commercial profit. Her dogs live full and active lives, and she says, 'I enjoy seeing my dogs running across open fields as much as I do showing them.'

She describes the cocker spaniel as 'a lot of dog in a compact body'.

We are greeted by three very noisy adult dogs, who set each other off in a cacophony of barking. They don't mean any harm but they're a very effective alarm system. Pat takes us past the display of rosettes covering one wall (that's just this year's haul) into the kitchen where the cupboards are full of china and porcelain cocker spaniel statuettes. I notice that she is wearing a dog-shaped necklace, and of course, it's a cocker spaniel.

After about ten minutes, the dogs settle down into their beds which are close to the kitchen island. They have accepted us into their home but are keeping an eye on us, just in case.

Two of them are boys and one is the bitch who has had the litter of puppies. She is having a break from the constant need to feed.

Pat tends to keep the dogs in the house rather than the bitches because – and don't tell them this – she likes the boys better.

The two who live with her have the run of the house and the others in the kennels require full-time care. Pat rises at 6am and is straight into the routine of feeding, exercising, grooming, cleaning out kennels, socialising puppies, feeding again, grooming some more and picking up poo. It's endless.

If there is a new litter of puppies, Pat won't go to bed at all for the first ten days in case the mother crushes one of them. She says with bigger litters, the mother can be so tired that she doesn't realise she has sat on one, so she makes it her duty to keep an eye on them all. That's ten days of fitful sleep on a sofa in the same room as the mother and her puppies.

This woman will do anything for her dogs.

Alice came with me to see Pat on the understanding that she would be allowed to cuddle a puppy, but I don't want to seem too keen and I am determined to ask sensible questions before we see the puppies. We ask all about the breed, its strengths and weaknesses, and how she is trying to breed better and better dogs.

Alice is obsessed with their ears. She remembers that her friend Bunker the springer spaniel used to get his long ears in his food when he ate. He quite enjoyed sucking them later for a tasty treat. She asks Pat how she copes with this problem and immediately we are offered a demonstration of her creative use of a snood. Apparently the dogs know that 'the snood means food' so they queue up to get them put on their ears before their tea.

Rolex (a good name for a dog) is called out and comes back wearing a shiny red snood around his ears. He looks as if he's about to ski down a mountain or ride a bicycle in the wind. Think Wallace and Gromit. The snood offers full protection for the ears from any food or water and not only will it keep him clean, it will allow those lovely long feathers to grow out at the end.

Pat and I also talk about responsible breeding, and that's the subject that gets her really animated. We are not here to take home a puppy – honestly, we're not – but if we were, we would be set the equivalent of an entrance exam. She wants to know that her puppies are going to a home that will be fully conscious of its needs and will be there at all times.

She is a member of the Kennel Club Assured Breeders scheme, which means that her kennels are inspected every three years and her breeding record is tracked and recorded, but it doesn't require prospective owners to be inspected. Pat does that bit for herself.

Honestly, I think she cares more about where her puppies will spend their lives than most parents care about where their children are going to school or who they will marry.

'I have taken a puppy out of the arms of a woman as she was about to leave and handed her the cheque back,' she says defiantly. Alice and I both look horrified and ask her why. 'She said she worked part-time and when I asked her what that really meant she said she was in the office three or four days a week. Well, that's not conducive to feeding a puppy four times a day so I'm sorry, I said, you're not having her.'

We asked how the prospective owner coped.

'She knew she'd been economical with the truth and although she was upset, she did understand. Unlike another family who threatened to sue me for defamation because I told them they weren't suitable dog owners.'

Pat tells us these things with a completely straight face. I'm not sure she appreciates that the world doesn't usually work like that. Hurrah for Pat, I say. She's fighting the corner for the dogs, not for stupid people, however rich and fancy they might be.

Her first two questions are whether the person has a secure garden and whether someone will be at home all day, every day, and believe me, you don't want to tell Pat a mistruth. She'll find out soon enough. I'd want Pat on my side in any argument about dogs. She's fearless and she's steadfast.

This is how breeders should be; you don't get that sort of rigorous interrogation if you're clicking a button to buy a puppy online. With online 'puppy shopping' comes real danger. First of all, puppy farms are being legitimised and protected by 'foster homes' that take the puppies and the bitch for the time that a prospective owner might visit. The buyer thinks they're seeing the puppies and the bitch in their natural environment but in fact she's been in a cage churning out litters of pups as often as possible.

Also, with no tracking system in place, inherent problems are being bred through generation after generation.

Talk to any vet and you will hear a litany of disaster stories about dogs that have issues so damaging that they have to be put down before they reach maturity. The family are left heartbroken. Also, if the pup is found to have a condition that is expensive to treat and the owners can't afford it, they have to give the dog to a rescue charity, which is equally painful and hard to explain to the children.

Breeders don't have to be registered with the Kennel Club. If puppies are being bred for the show ring, then both the sire and the dam have to be registered and so does the litter. Around 35,000 litters are registered each year and the numbers suggest that that only covers about 30 per cent of the dogs born in the UK.

The parliaments or assemblies of England, Wales, Scotland and Northern Ireland have slightly different rules but generally, anyone breeding three or more litters over a 12-month period and selling puppies or advertising that they sell puppies has to have a dog breeding licence. The intention is not to catch out hobby breeders who might have one litter once in a while; it is to crack down on puppy farms.

The Assured Breeders scheme has about 3,000 breeders listed and it's voluntary. That number is a mere fraction of those who are breeding dogs in this country. It's why we, the prospective owners, have to be much more vigilant about where we're sourcing any new dog. We should be asking to see a dog breeder's licence and if they don't have one, we need to know why. We also need to be a bit more savvy about prices. I know people who have paid upwards of £4,000 for a puppy because demand rose so much during lockdown.

If it's too easy to buy a puppy, then there's something wrong. The only way of stopping unscrupulous breeders from making as much money as they can with very little concern for dog health and wellbeing is not to buy from them.

'The responsible breeders are the ones who are doing all the health testing and are trying to improve and protect the breed,' Pat says. 'Whereas the "greeders", as we call them, just want to make money.'

I hadn't heard that word before, but it makes sense. When Pat started, the going rate for a puppy was £175. It is now £2,000, and many 'greeders' will charge more. Pat could have made a fortune if she were that way inclined, but instead she is breeding fewer litters than she used to.

'We have a responsibility to supply demand,' Pat argues. 'And the demand is very low right now because so many people got dogs during lockdown. The market is gridlocked and we should be very careful to not over-inflate the numbers.'

Pat makes sure that her vet sees all of her puppies a week before they go out to their new homes and makes it part of the contract with the new owner that their vet will see the puppy within seven days so that they have two independent assessments in order to pick up any issues. She always keeps the best puppy for showing, so she would rather all the others go to homes where they will be pets.

'The best owners are the ones who've just retired,' she says. 'They've waited all their lives to have time to have a dog and they're in no rush. I always ask myself whether a person can look after their puppy as well as I would. If they can, that's fine.'

She advises that a good breeder will always take a dog back if there's a problem. If you find your puppy has an allergy, an issue with its eyes, kidneys, joints or anything that causes them ongoing discomfort, you must report it back to the breeder and to the breed club so they have a record and can track issues in certain lines.

Every pedigree breed has a breed club which oversees the health and development of that breed. The Cocker Spaniel Club was founded in 1902 and has a health and welfare officer who can independently track inherited conditions and stop a breeder from perpetuating a damaging condition or trait.

'Every generation needs to be better than the last, and that gets harder as you go higher up,' Pat says. 'I'm breeding from champions so it's pretty hard to improve them, but that's the challenge.'

She breeds minority colours like black, white and tan, which gives her an interesting USP with her dogs. Her bitch Tangle looks up at us. She is mainly black and white but her eyebrows are tan and she has a little tan on her muzzle and on the ends of her ears. She is very pretty.

Alice is getting restless. She wants to see the puppies. Luckily, Pat can sense it and suggests we go out to meet them. On the way, she shows us her grooming room, complete with a swivel table so she can brush, trim, backcomb and spray both sides of a dog without problems. I have seen fancy London hair salons with fewer products than Pat's grooming room.

She tries to groom the dogs daily or at least every other day because she says if you leave it today, you've just got to deal with a bigger problem tomorrow. Their hair matts very easily and needs constant attention. It's also good practice to put your hands on your dog every day to check for any lumps or bumps, as well as brushing them. It takes two hours to prepare each dog for the show ring on competition days.

We used to send Archie to the groomers every six weeks. His hair cost more to cut than mine, and he loved it. Like the vet's, they gave him treats so he was always happy to go in. They trimmed his coat, his nails, sorted out his anal glands (I'd have taken on the rest, but not that) and gave him a good wash and blow-dry. Once they trimmed his legs too short and they looked like twigs, but apart from that one mistake, they did a great job. He always came out with a little red bow on his collar. They told us that was because he'd been a good boy. It took us years to work out that every dog got a little bow when they'd been finished. To be honest, I was a bit crushed. I thought he was the star pupil, but it turns out he was just the same as every other dog. Ah well, at least he hadn't bitten anyone.

Past Pat's grooming salon, we go through another gate and we can hear squeaking.

We see little black and white faces on the other side of a metal mesh door and they start screaming in desperation to meet us. When Pat opens the door, eight little pups spill over the step and come waddling towards us, their tails wagging. They are squeaking with every step and almost immediately they stop to have a pee. I wait for them to finish all that before I scoop one up for a cuddle. Otherwise there's a danger of them peeing on your leg, which is never a good thing before a long drive home.

There is nothing like the smell, the feel, the warmth of puppies. They have fat little pink tummies and coats as soft as silk. I am lost in the heaven of puppy love.

Alice points at one of the larger ones with a lot of white on his head and lower-set black markings on his cheeks and his neck. He looks more contained and calmer than the others.

'He's lovely,' she says. 'I like him.'

'That's the one I'm keeping,' Pat replies. 'He's called Time.'

Alice looks proud as punch. She can select a winning show dog, all right. I have picked up one of the smaller ones, who immediately nestles into my neck and starts sucking on my ear lobe. It's lovely, if a little noisy, until I feel a sharp prick and realise that I may be about to get an additional ear piercing that I don't want.

I put the puppy down and he butts his head into one of his siblings. She immediately pees on him.

That's the way life rolls when you're a seven-week-old puppy. One minute you're having a lovely cuddle, the next your sister is peeing on your head.

My brother always claims I was mean to him, but as far I can recall, I never did *that*.

The puppies are rolling around on the gravel, play-fighting with each other. Pat keeps jumping up to scoop up poo. It's better than a Pilates workout. Up she gets and scoop. Sit down and cuddle. Up again and scoop before they tread in it. Down again and cuddle.

She says she can spend all day doing this and it's her idea of bliss. I can see what she means.

The puppies are all off to their new homes in a week or so. The new owners have been thoroughly vetted and approved and will be getting the most adorable, loyal and loving dogs with whom to share their lives.

It was a real treat to have a little taste of that character with the latest generation of Ryallcourt cocker spaniels. All of the puppies had designated homes so there was no chance of us reserving one for ourselves, but it was mighty tempting. I remember the first weeks that Archie was with us as a puppy and I spent many nights sleeping downstairs on the sofa beside him so that he wouldn't get lonely. I would be happy to go through all of that again in return for that gorgeous smell when you cuddle a puppy. There is nothing better.

CHAPTER 10

Dog Shows and
Other Showbiz Pursuits

I have no doubt that the puppy who stays behind with Pat will be a champion, and expect to see Ryallcourt Step in Time, to give him his full title, in future years at Crufts. Pat discovered showing back in 1988 and it soon became an obsession. She has bred six cocker spaniel champions in four different colours.

As Jessica explained, breeding good show dogs is part science, part art. You get the best-looking, healthiest dog (who is not related to your bitch) and make sure that what he has will complement what your bitch has. If she is a little big, he should be small; if she has a narrow chest, he should have a wide one; and so on.

Get the cross right and you end up with puppies who have all the best bits of their parents and none of the worst bits. Then it's down to the breeder to keep that puppy in the best possible condition, feed it correctly, exercise it just enough but not too much, groom it and teach it to stand for a judge, to walk with elegance around the ring and to enjoy the experience of a day at a dog show.

Crufts, of course, is the biggest show of them all. In 2023 it welcomed over 24,000 dogs, with over 200 breeds (around 30 per group) competing to be Best in Show. It's a marathon of an event, so only the very fittest in mind and body will succeed. On the final evening, the seven group winners go up against each other.

How do you compare a miniature wirehaired dachshund to a Bernese mountain dog or a boxer to a papillon? The answer is that the judge has to assess each dog against the breed standard and the closest to perfection wins the prize. I guess it's a bit like the Chelsea Flower Show, where gardens are judged against their plans, or *The Great British Bake Off* where a cake or a bread is meant to be a certain way and not have a soggy bottom. There is always the added element of the X factor, of course, and sometimes you can see that a dog has a certain special quality, like Orca the lagotto romagnolo who won Best in Show in 2023, that makes it shine.

Some of them rise to the occasion of the final evening with a packed arena, spotlights, music and the overwhelming aroma of nervous tension. Others shrink from it and disappear into themselves. The best handlers know exactly how to relax their dog, when to groom and when to leave them alone. It's a show, after all, and it's about performance as much as looks.

Puppies can compete at shows from six to twelve months of age, then they move into junior classes until they are eighteen months old. It's everyone against each other from then on until they get to seven years old when they go into veteran classes. A good handler will make sure their dog is switched on and ready to perform when it comes to his or her turn but there's no point tiring them out by keeping them too buzzy all day long.

Lots of dogs go to ringcraft classes so they get used to the idea of parading around a ring with other dogs and being held in position for the judge. More experienced handlers might set up a ring at home and practise with a young dog so it gets comfortable running on the lead alongside or in front of its handler. No one wants to see a dog getting dragged around the ring.

Small dogs are lifted up and shown on a table. Larger dogs are examined on the ground and it's important that they get used to having a stranger's hands all over their body and in their mouth, looking at their teeth. A dog needs to be comfortable with the whole process; if they are nervous or aggressive, they'll be penalised. If a dog bites the judge, it is immediately disqualified.

I was given a book called *Dog Showing: From Beginners to Winners* by Robert Killick. He quotes an eminent judge as saying 'Dog Showing should be fun; dog breeding is serious.' Killick notes that 'some people become so obsessed with winning at dog shows that they get upset and quite bitter if they do not succeed. This is not only foolish but also counterproductive. Showing your dog should be fun, so don't let it get to you.'

When we were visiting Pat's spaniels, Alice asked her whether the dog showing world is as cut-throat as she imagines.

'Oh, the competition is hideous,' Pat concedes. 'But out of the ring we all have the dogs' best interests at heart.'

In case we think she doesn't like her fellow competitors she adds quickly: 'I've met some wonderful people all over the world.'

Alice and I looked at each other. Hmm. We're not sure this is an environment we would enjoy. I've never trusted judged sports as much as outright matches or races.

When I used to do dressage as part of my teenage obsession with eventing, I always thought the judge was biased against me. In truth, I just wasn't very good at dressage. However, I now own half a horse (to clarify, the horse is whole and unharmed) with Harry Meade, whose riding is beyond reproach, and I get similarly upset when the judge doesn't appreciate the beauty and elegance of our horse above all others. It isn't a fair fight.

So imagine if your dog is in the show ring and you know he or she is perfect in every way and the judge doesn't give you the winning ticket? That's torture. Especially if the ticket goes to a fierce rival.

I'm not sure either Alice or I have the right temperament for it. We'd be those bitter, angry folk Robert Killick was warning against. We might end up cornering the judge and not letting them go until they explain exactly why they made the decision they made.

Mind you, I think that does happen at some shows. That's why I would equally never be a judge – again.

I agreed to judge at the Kingsclere dog show one year. It was one of the biggest mistakes I have ever made. Believe me, there is no quicker way to make an enemy of everyone in the village, apart from the one owner to whom you give the trophy.

Judging 'Best Trick' was easy though. There was a Labrador who came into the ring with a small child on the end of its lead. After about a minute it decided there were more interesting things going on at the hamburger stand so it took off, taking the child flying with it. The child was in tears and howling in pain, having been dragged for 100 metres across a graveyard (the show was at the church).

I felt sorry for the child so I pretended it was a stunt trick worthy of Gill Raddings and gave her the winning rosette. It didn't stop her crying.

So, I get it. Judging is hard. But it's true that some judges are not always completely unbiased (that's putting it politely) and that people will withdraw their dogs from certain competitions before they even start if they think the judge is set against them.

I'm distracted by memories of *Best in Show*, which if you like dogs and have ever seen a dog show, is a must-watch. Co-written and starring Christopher Guest (*This is Spinal Tap*) and Eugene Levy (of *Schitt's Creek* fame), it is a mockumentary about the fictitious Mayflower Dog Show in Philadelphia. It has a terrific cast including Jane Lynch (coach Sue Sylvester in

Glee) and Jennifer Coolidge (Tanya in *The White Lotus*), whose characters end up having an affair with each other.

I was advised not to watch it until *after* I presented Crufts for the first time in 2004. It is full of eccentric dog owners primping, preening, back-stabbing, having secret affairs, attempting to influence judges and being bad losers or crowing winners.

It has an idiot TV presenter making inane, ill-informed comments about the different breeds. I think that's why I had to wait until after I'd presented Crufts once, in case I followed the same path. It's very funny but the advice was well heeded.

Although dedicated to the art of showing, Pat knows that her showing dog doesn't know whether it's won or not because she treats them all just the same.

'Even if the judge doesn't give them a winning ticket, I know I'm still taking the best dog home.'

That's the attitude to have if you're going to have a long and successful career in dog showing. You can't win all the time, even if you think you should, so you've got to love your dogs to bits and there is no doubt that Pat does.

'It really is a wonderful breed that I am privileged to share my life with.'

* * *

I collected many injuries as a child and I was proud of them. Lots of scars on my knees, a great scar on my foot where I stuck a pitchfork through it, a small scar in the centre of my hand where I was chiselling a piece of wood with great vigour and slipped off the wood into my palm (that didn't, as you know already, put me off carpentry) and the obligatory scar below my mouth from where my teeth went through. That was a result of banging my head on a basin. I think it was my brother Andrew's fault. I'm sure I blamed him, even if it wasn't.

As for broken bones, I think I got off fairly lightly: a broken collarbone at two years old falling off Valkyrie, a broken finger that was slammed in a stable door and a broken toe that was acquired while attempting to teach the dogs to do agility.

Andrew and I raided the rotting and decrepit 'summer house' that was full of junk like ancient croquet sets, old doors and wardrobes, kept just in case.

Just in case of what I have no idea, but I have a suspicion that my mother is a borderline hoarder. She really doesn't like to throw anything away. She still has our school reports, old toys, sheets from the 1970s and towels that are so crunchy even the dogs don't want to be dried with them.

'Waste not, want not,' she says, although I think I'd want a new set of towels.

When our parents built a new house, Mum kept the windows of the old house in the garage. I'm not talking about lovely Victorian sash windows. I mean crap 1970s windows.

'You never know when it might come in handy,' Mum says.

I'm prepared to put money on the *never* bit of that sentence. Mind you, I've just been out to our garden shed to retrieve the sensor that's meant to scare the foxes away and I've found four large stone slabs leaning up against the wall, a box of tiles left over from when the shower was installed and some grey slate floor tiles. All bound to be useful. As for the fox sensor, it's useless. We never used to have a problem with foxes when we had Archie but for the last two years we've had a family of fox cubs in our garden. They're very sweet when they're little but when they start jumping all over the furniture, destroying the plants, digging holes in the lawn and peeing on the cushions, I am less enamoured.

I suppose I could get all of those tiles out and lay them around the place. That might work, and it's the sort of second-hand use of which my mother would approve. Thinking of which, I'm pretty sure she admired us using the old doors from the summer house to build an agility course for the dogs. I don't know for sure because we didn't ask. We thought we'd do it as a surprise and impress her by showing off the dogs' new skills.

Andrew and I dragged out the wooden doors, along with old brooms and garden shovels, runner bean stakes to make bending poles and an old tractor tyre that stood up on its own. With an hour's hard labour, we had designed our own show-jumping course for the dogs.

I was so excited when we'd finished and couldn't wait to share it with Polly and Jenny the lurchers as well as Lily the boxer. I had seen dog agility on the telly, so I knew exactly what to do and started to order my younger brother around with a great deal of authority. Nothing new there, he would like me to point out, and I would like to say that there's nothing new in the fact that he didn't listen.

The big problem we had was the dogs.

They sat there staring at us as if we were mad. We called and cajoled and tried treats but they didn't seem to know what to do, so we decided we'd better show them. I ran ahead of Andrew, calling him to follow so that the dogs would understand what they were meant to do. We jumped the obstacles, twisted ourselves in and out of the runner bean stakes, crawled through the tyre and ran through the finish line. The dogs sat and stared. It was almost as if they were laughing at us.

'Let's do it again,' I shouted at Andrew. 'They'll get the hang of it this time.'

I would love to tell you that I leap over fences like a gazelle, but I don't. I jump as you might imagine an elephant would jump. There is nothing elegant or athletic about it. As my concentration was diverted towards the bemused dogs, it's not surprising that I banged a large white door, sending it crashing down, and somehow I got my foot trapped under it. It was agony.

I broke my big toe and bruised the top of my foot so badly that I couldn't wear shoes or boots for a week. I ordered my brother to clear up the course, citing injury, and hobbled back to the house hoping that my mother wouldn't come out and find her precious junk all over the lawn.

The dogs scampered alongside me, delighted to be let off the hook. I had clearly confirmed their suspicion that the show-jumping course we had designed was dangerous and stupid.

That was my first experience of dog agility. It may not surprise you to learn that I didn't try again.

I do, however, love watching the experts do it properly.

Dog agility has become a massive part of the entertainment in the main arena at Crufts. It was introduced in 1978 by a member of the organising committee called John Varley. Based on the idea of show jumping for horses, it combined the basic tenets of obedience with speed and excitement. It was an instant hit and soon the courses became more difficult with ramps, tunnels, weaving poles, a see-saw, tight turns and switchbacks.

As I appreciate that it's not easy to train dogs to follow a course of even basic jumps, I thought I'd better talk to someone who is quite good at it.

I've known Charlotte Baker since she was a youngster because her father, Clifford, is head lad to record-breaking 14-times champion jumps trainer Paul Nicholls. Clifford was the man who used to ride dual Cheltenham Gold Cup winner Kauto Star in the mornings and has been a key part of the success of the team at Ditcheat stables.

Charlotte, meanwhile, is a rising star of the British agility world. It all started when she was just 13 years old and had a puppy who is a cockapoo crossed with a rare American breed called a miki. It was not a planned mating but one of those lucky mistakes that can happen in a kennels where dogs are being bred. The gorgeous outcome was Buddy, who is a bright-eyed, black and white, soft-furred bundle of affection.

Charlotte took Buddy to puppy classes and started to do some basic training around obedience and general manners. By chance, the puppy class trainer mentioned agility and Charlotte thought she'd give it a go.

'I just loved it because Buddy loved it,' she tells me. 'He was so willing to learn and he picked things up so quickly. It helps exercise the dog and keeps you fit, but the thing that made me fall in love with it is the bond that you get with your dog through doing it. You have to be a team and work together as a partnership.'

Through the modern wonders of Facebook, Instagram and WhatsApp, Charlotte connected with other fans of agility and found out more about the various competitions and training clubs around the country. With her mother, Sarah, driving her to all sorts of venues, she was soon hooked.

'It's such a lovely community. It's very inclusive – all ages of people, all sorts of breeds of dogs. When we go to dog shows, everyone just loves dogs and loves agility and wants to be out there having fun. They're all there for the same reason.'

Charlotte now handles a team of dogs with Buddy still going strong, a young bearded collie called Blaze and a lovely bearded collie called Eliza, who was originally run by Ashleigh Butler.

If you're thinking you recognise that name, you would be right. It's the same Ashleigh Butler who won *Britain's Got Talent* in 2012 dancing with her dog Pudsey.

To be technically correct in dog language, they were doing heelwork to music but 'the dancing dog' is how the act was sold to the TV public. Pudsey was the competition's first animal winner and head judge Simon Cowell, who had long wanted a dog act to succeed, claimed, 'My life's work is now complete.'

Pudsey became a star of stage and screen, as well as securing a book deal and various advertising slots. He was an A-list celebrity and probably the most famous and successful British canine star of the 21st century.

Pudsey died in 2017, but Ashleigh has continued to centre her life around dogs and is a regular competitor in agility and heelwork to music. She has been a mentor to Charlotte, who had asked her for advice on how to get the best out of her young dog, Blaze. She went for a lesson with Ashleigh and loved it. A little later, Ashleigh asked Charlotte if she would consider competing with Eliza because she didn't have the time to commit to her fully. She said she thought they would be a good match.

Charlotte and Eliza started to compete regularly together and soon it became clear that they were bonded. Ashleigh asked Charlotte if she would like to take Eliza on full time.

'I cried when she asked me if I wanted Eliza to live with us because I knew it was such a massive thing for her and a very unselfish thing to do,' Charlotte says. 'She is a very loyal dog and Ashleigh knew that she would be even better in competition if she knew I was fully committed to her. It's worked out really well.'

Charlotte's dream was to compete at Crufts and in 2023, she and Eliza made it to the Championship Final for medium dogs. At the age of 19, Charlotte was the youngest competitor in the class. She finished third.

It was a huge achievement and although she is usually very calm about competition, she admits that it was the first time she had ever really felt nervous. She couldn't sleep the night before and kept thinking she was going to be sick.

'I just didn't want to let Eliza down because everyone knows she's a brilliant dog and I didn't want to let Ashleigh down. I didn't want to fall over or look stupid and it's the first time I've ever felt like that. Luckily it was OK.'

I tell her it was more than OK. As they set off at speed, Eliza was locked on to the challenges ahead. She leaped over coloured show jumps, turned on a sixpence to the next obstacle, carefully negotiated the see-saw where the dogs have to put their paws on the white-painted areas at the start and the end, weaved her way so fast through the weaving poles that she was a blur, scampered through the tunnel and raced her way over the finish line. She hadn't made a single mistake, and as she jumped into Charlotte's arms, they both knew they'd done the very best they could do.

'It makes me emotional just thinking about it,' she admits. 'I really wanted my first time in the main arena to be with Eliza. She's such a special dog and the way she looks at me on the start line just melts my heart every time.'

Ashleigh was watching on proudly, cheering them every step of the way. Her magnanimous and generous decision to let Eliza live with Charlotte has transformed them both. Eliza is achieving her potential in the ring and Charlotte is blossoming into a top-class competitor and a more confident person.

'I love having her by my side,' she says of Eliza. 'She's such a joy in life. I knew she could do it but I didn't think I'd ever get into a Championship Final. It was a fairytale day and it was amazing to be amongst those people who I've looked up to for years in such a prestigious class. She was awesome and it was everything I've ever dreamt of.'

Charlotte has just finished an animal management course at college and is planning to do an Open University degree so that she can study around her commitments to her dogs. During the summer, she tends to be competing every weekend and she certainly wouldn't dream of going abroad for a break without her dogs. She competes internationally so treats that as a holiday, and it's clear she is living a life full of joyful energy. Her mother is a key part of it all and is right there whenever Charlotte needs her.

'I don't drive yet, so my mum takes me to pretty much every competition and it's lovely to spend time with her. My dad doesn't get a lot of time off, but he comes when he can and that's great. He's been really interesting with information from the racing world that might help me with the dogs. There are a lot of similarities between the sports, and we talk about nutrition and fitness.'

Although technically not a sport, I think Charlotte's correct in referring to it as such. It is, for now, completely amateur, with no prize money and only the occasional reward but it's a competitive environment that requires physical fitness, commitment to training and mental strength. There have been calls for dog agility to be included in the Olympics. It's an interesting idea. For now, Charlotte is happy with how it works and even happier with the effect it has had on her.

'It's opened up another part of me that I didn't even know existed,' she says. 'I went from this shy thirteen-year-old who wouldn't even speak to being able to talk to anyone. I've made some lifelong friends and that's huge because I didn't really have loads of friends growing up and I didn't want to go out to parties, but now I'm constantly surrounded by people who love their dogs and just want to be with their dogs.

'That forty seconds I get in the ring with them gives me such a buzz. When I gave up riding I didn't know what I wanted to do, but agility fast went from being a hobby to being my life. It's saved me. It's given me something to focus on and I get to spend all my time with dogs I adore. It's definitely changed my life for the better.'

So, the next time you watch the dog agility at Crufts or at the Christmas International Show that I still call Olympia even though it's not held there any more, think about the relationship between the dogs and their owners and how much it means to them all to be a successful team working in harmony.

* * *

The basic obedience and physical dexterity that is required to be successful in agility can be a great crossover skill. Gill Raddings has competed at the highest level with her Belgian shepherd dogs and was part of the team that won the World Championships in 2005. She also happens to be the leading agent for stunt dogs in the UK and one of the most respected trainers in the business.

Oh yes, there are stunt dogs. Gill has been running her business, Stunt Dogs and Animals, for 25 years, and has supplied dogs to TV series like *Doc Martin* (the grumpy doctor's Jack Russell, Buddy), *Poldark* and *Midsomer Murders*, and films like *Spider-Man: Far from Home*, *Wonder Woman 1984* and *Bohemian Rhapsody*.

It's not only dogs on her books; Gill and her team of animal trainers can also supply cats, cows, ducks, reindeer, goats, rats, pigs, birds and even bugs if required. Intrigued by the very idea of this, I went to visit her at her home in Oxfordshire.

The first thing I notice is the customised minivan outside the front door. It has four individual sections in the back with deep, soft blankets inside and a big open space right behind the driver's seat for a bigger dog. There are leads hanging from hooks, a basket of rubber toys, a large container of dog food and plenty of bowls stacked up. This is the official Winnebago for the canine performers. I'm impressed.

'Are you ready?' Gill says to me as she prepares to open the front door.

I nod. I am expecting a whole coterie of animals to attack me but in fact it's just three dogs, one of which she is minding for the neighbours.

I am enthusiastically greeted by two terriers called Bree and Widget and a beautiful long-haired Belgian shepherd dog (Tervuren) called Yara. They all bark hello, jump up and want a fuss.

They all look familiar and it's not surprising. These are A-list celebrities of the dog world.

Remember Wellard in *EastEnders*? That was Gill's dog. He is long gone but has been followed by a long list of star dogs. She has grown used to the world of film and television where people are not always as nice as their characters on screen might suggest. The dogs see through them.

'You can always tell a genuine dog lover from the actors who are just tolerating them,' she says. 'And my word, the dogs can tell.'

We take a cup of coffee into the sitting room where the sofas are covered in blankets and immediately the dogs jump up and climb all over me. I hope I've passed the test of being a real dog lover.

Widget is a rescue dog who is currently starring in a major commercial while Bree (who has one blue eye) is a Jack Russell with a very distinctive look. Widget and Bree have one end of a toy each and are pulling it apart. They are very proud of their attempted murder display.

The shelves are lined with trophies from agility classes and the walls decorated with rosettes. The wall outside by the staircase is crammed with photos of Gill and her dogs. Her upstairs study, where she takes care of all the bookings, has another sofa with a loose cover so that the dogs can come to the office with her and be comfortable.

Gill started off with horses but when she first got a Tervuren she started doing canine tracking and obedience work and then took up agility. Her dog won Police Dog of the Year. As Gill is talking about her first dog, Yara lifts one of her paws and puts it across her eye. She looks at Gill as if she is embarrassed or ashamed. I wonder if she can understand even more than we realise. Gill reads my mind and assures me that it's her favourite trick and she does it for attention, not because she disapproves of us talking about another dog.

'I'm always amazed at how much you can teach a dog to do and how much they understand,' she says.

I tell her a story I heard about a Chihuahua that came from a pound in Florida. The new owner had been assured that she was obedient and knew all sorts of commands. The woman tried the basics like sit, stay and called her name. She responded to her name but looked blank at all the other requests. The woman assumed she had been spun a lie until a friend asked whether perhaps the dog didn't understand English.

'There are a lot of Spanish speakers in Florida,' the friend pointed out. 'Why don't you try Spanish?'

The woman laughed but decided to give it a go. The Chihuahua was transformed. She understood and obeyed every command.

I know that some police forces deliberately train their dogs in another language so that they can't be thrown off track by somebody else shouting a command in English.

Gill always makes sure her dogs are trained to obey visual commands as well as verbal ones.

I ask how on earth she trains them to do so many complicated things and she offers to show me.

'I do most of the training in here because the studios are often quite confined and they need to be able to work in small, busy spaces,' she explains. 'I back everything up with a hand signal because there are lots of times when the actor has dialogue and the dog needs to do something on command but I can't do it verbally.'

She shuts the two terriers out of the room so that Yara can focus, and places a small square tile on the ground. She explains that the first thing she does is train the dogs to stand on a mark, so that on set they can be in the right position for cameras and lighting and be guaranteed to stay there. If only human actors could be so reliable.

Yara is immediately onto her mark and staring at Gill for instruction. She's keen and willing. Gill has a special bag of frankfurters that are only used for training. They are the tastiest of pay cheques for a working dog. She shows me how she can alter Yara's eyeline with a piece of sausage on the end of an extendable wand (it looks like a car aerial from an old car) so that the dog could look from one person to another or stare at a point in the distance if required.

She asks Yara to roll over, to crawl along the floor, to limp, to walk backwards, to hide her head and, the old favourite, to cover one eye. Yara does everything as the command is barely out of Gill's mouth. If she was a sprinter, she'd be leaping out of the starting blocks on the B of the Bang.

I am amazed at how fast and how completely she has transformed from that soppy pet playing on the sofa to a fully committed, totally focused professional. I can see why she's in high demand.

'I have to say I still get a kick out of seeing my own dogs on TV,' Gill says. 'They're very clever and they can learn hundreds of words and loads of different tricks.'

I ask whether her dogs ever recognise themselves on TV and I'm a little bit disappointed when she says no. Maybe I shouldn't have taken it so personally that Archie never registered me on the telly. It's clearly a medium that doesn't give the dog the key things it needs – smell and aura.

The demonstration over, the wooden tile is hidden behind a cushion and Yara goes back to being a pet.

A bit like Charlotte Baker with her agility, Gill loves the connection and the bond she gets with her dogs through training. She works with loads of different breeds and often trains other people's dogs. She manages their acting careers, paying the owners for the days their dog is working.

'A good dog can earn a lot of money over its lifetime but it only works if they enjoy the job. You can't make a dog do things it doesn't want to do.'

She has clear no-go zones. She turned down a valuable commercial because it involved a dog having its teeth cleaned with human toothpaste. Even though the company explained that it would actually be dog toothpaste, she said it didn't matter because the advert was giving the impression that it was human toothpaste, which is poisonous to dogs, and she wouldn't condone that messaging. She also turned down an advert that involved a stick being thrown for a puppy, even if they used a toy that looked like a stick. It's never a good idea to throw a stick for a dog because of the danger of splinters in the mouth or choking.

'People are easily influenced,' she says. 'And they believe what they see on the television. I can't be involved in promoting things that are dangerous or wrong.'

Gill also loves working with farm animals and has provided pigs, goats, sheep and cows for film work; she tells me that pigs are particularly intelligent and trainable. But it's dogs to whom she has dedicated most of her life.

'I can normally tell as soon as a dog comes through the front door whether or not it's going to work. They've got to be confident in themselves, friendly to other dogs, not nervous of people or noise and they have to be food driven.'

Bree and Widget are back in the sitting room now, furious that they have missed out on the action.

As we are speaking, Yara and Bree are play-fighting on the sofa next to Gill. Their jaws are wide open and Bree has her whole head in Yara's mouth. There is not a hint of aggression in their behaviour; they're just having fun. They have total trust in each other.

It confirms my belief that dogs want to work. They love to learn new tricks and they always want to please.

CHAPTER 11

Goodwoof, West Sussex

I know there are people in the world whose life will not be complete unless they go to Glastonbury. It's on everyone's bucket list. Well, not everyone's, because it's not on mine.

I'm happy to watch on TV but I don't need to be there. Alice is equally unmoved by the prospect of camping in a muddy field in the hope of seeing a band play on a distant stage. She says she wants warm running water, a bed with sheets on it and a good view, thank you very much.

I don't mind literary festivals and I quite like the idea of walking festivals, but my favourite concept is the increasingly popular dog festival. To my mind, a festival can't be 'fun for all the family' unless it embraces dogs.

All outdoor horse events are dog friendly, but they seldom have activities and treatments just for dogs. That's why we need weekends with names like DogFest, Paws in the Park, Big Doggie Do and Dogstival. They must have been very pleased when they came up those titles but the best I have seen is the equally well-named Goodwoof.

I have been to Goodwood races since I was little and I've always loved it. It's a beautiful downland course in West Sussex with open countryside as far as the eye can see. The grandstand looks like a series of Arthurian jousting tents or the sails of a ship with its curved white roofs.

I rode there as an amateur jockey and even had a winner or two, but my clearest memory is finishing fourth on a horse who didn't try very hard and getting shouted at by a punter who clearly didn't think I had made enough effort. He didn't know that if I'd have picked up my stick, I'd have probably fallen off and the horse most certainly would have gone backwards.

When someone has had a bet, you can't reason with them, so I smiled at him and patted my horse on the neck.

In the decades after that, I presented Glorious Goodwood over five days every summer for both the BBC and Channel 4 and, to my relief, didn't get shouted at by anyone, except the producer if I did something he wasn't expecting. It was one of the highlights of my career as a racing broadcaster because it combined top-class racing with a lovely, relaxed atmosphere. The men wear panamas and linen suits while the women glide around in floaty dresses and floppy hats. It has a very earthy, rural feel with more picnics than sit-down lunches. It's a tricky course that often produces dramatic finishes, and in good weather, I cannot think of a more scenically beautiful sporting setting anywhere in the world.

The history of Goodwood is fascinating. Owned by the Dukes of Richmond since 1697, it has always been an estate with sport at its heart.

The first Duke – the illegitimate son of Charles II – rented and then bought Goodwood to indulge his love of hunting. Interestingly, for anyone who loves an OS map (like me), the third Duke of Richmond was Master of the Ordnance and instrumental in the project to map the whole of Britain at one inch to the mile. This later became the Ordnance Survey and is the reason that we have better maps of footpaths and bridleways than any other country in the world. It was also the third Duke who founded the racecourse, built the magnificent stables and, as a keen huntsman, loved his hounds so much that he built them their own stately home.

In 1787, he commissioned the renowned Georgian architect James Wyatt to build an elaborate and beautiful kennels. The kennels is now the clubhouse for the golf club and I'm telling you, there are manor houses that do not come up to the standards of that building. It was and still is magnificent.

The hounds had their own lodges with access to open-air courtyards. They had their own chef and, most impressively, their own heating system. Large iron plates outside the walls were heated with giant fires to send warmth through the walls to keep the dogs comfortable in winter. In effect, the kennels had central heating about a hundred years before the humans at Goodwood House. It was dubbed 'the most luxurious doghouse in the world' and it is the perfect backdrop for Goodwoof, the modern celebration of dogs.

Inspired by the family's love of dogs, Goodwoof is the latest festival on the Goodwood Estate. The current Duke of Richmond is a great believer in doing things that fit in with the historic family passions. His mother was a big fan of dressage and carriage driving, so Goodwood has hosted international events for both. His grandfather, the ninth Duke, was keen on motor racing and built one of the most respected motor racing circuits in the world, host of the first big professional event after the Second World War. For 16 years the Goodwood Circuit was known as the spiritual home of British motor racing and in 1998, the current duke founded the Goodwood Revival to celebrate the cars and the fashions of that era. Then they added the Goodwood Festival of Speed, which makes use of the hillclimb track to give the petrolheads a chance to let rip. I am not a car aficionado, but I have friends who are and they are devoted to the Goodwood Revival and Festival of Speed. All the top names in Formula One want to be there and it's a rare chance for the public to mingle with their heroes.

The duke's mission in founding Goodwoof in 2022 was to create something that had space, variety and was a joyful but relaxed celebration of all the things that make dogs special.

In 2023 it cost £35 per adult to get in to Goodwoof, which includes all the events, veterinary checks and advice, behaviour training and DNA tests for your dog. Children under 12 get in for free. There is seating everywhere on straw bales, benches, deckchairs or picnic tables, and plenty of food and drink outlets. They've made sure there is lots of shade and water stations which, on a warm spring day, are essential.

I was impressed by the scale of the festival and the atmosphere it generated. Given that this is a very new event, they have already achieved impressive numbers: more than 18,000 people came through the gates in its second year. There must have been more than 10,000 dogs.

Dogs are big business. British dog owners spend an average of £2,136 a year on their dogs, not including dog care or veterinary costs. That covers food, toys, dog beds, chews and outfits. Yes, outfits. One in five dog owners spends £20 a month on outfits for their dog. It's never really been my thing but Archie did once have a jumper for the winter. He refused to walk in it and we had to take it off.

Food was more his thing so he was a large personal contributor to the British dog food industry, which is worth over £1.5 billion a year. Globally, the pet industry is worth $260 billion. There was plenty of shopping to be done at Goodwoof but of course, rather than call it a shopping zone, it's the ReTail Area with lots of independent traders selling sustainable, eco-friendly goods and toys made of recycled rubber. There is also a Pawtrait area where you can get a professional photo of your dog curated by a canine art gallery.

I talked to all sorts of people and met all sorts of breeds. Everyone was united by one thing: the love of dogs. There were all sorts of activities and talks and I was even brave enough to read an extract from this book to the audience at Literary Corner. When the dogs barked at the end, I interpreted it as approval.

I love the questions I get at book readings and one of my favourites this time was, 'If you were a dog, which breed would you be?' I thought about it.

I'm energetic and friendly, certainly not sleek or elegant like a hound, I like my food, I'm good at sleeping and I'm not very obedient. As I was going through my characteristics and the canine equivalents, someone shouted from behind me: 'Boxer!'

Of course. I shouldn't have over-thought it: I would be a boxer. Hopefully a bit better behaved than Mum's Boris, but a boxer through and through.

Another child put up their hand and asked me if I knew what a bracco Italiano was. Now that's a good test. My brain clicked into over-drive and I suddenly remembered going down the line of gundogs at Crufts. There was one who looked more like a basset hound than a gundog. That was it – the brown and tan bracco Italiano with the long ears and the droopy face. I described it as best I could and said, 'They're very good at smelling things out – are they an Italian pointer?'

'Yes!' she said, clearly delighted.

Phew. Sometimes setting yourself up as a dog expert can be fraught with danger.

At the book signing after my talk, a woman came forward with her Labrador. She explained that they were about to take off in a camper van on a walking tour of the UK.

'He's saved me,' she said, pointing at her dog. I looked at her and wondered why. I didn't want to ask in case she thought I was prying, but in the space of silence, as so often happens, she filled me in.

'My husband died,' she said. 'It was very unexpected and I promise you, if it wasn't for this boy here, I don't know what I would have done.'

Her dog had given her love, companionship but most of all a reason to get up in the morning and try to carry on. She was getting through each day because of him and as the weeks and months went on, she realised that he was an important connection to her husband and that together, they could go on adventures that would allow her to remember.

I have spoken to many people over the years who use walking as a way of navigating bereavement. The very act of putting one foot in front of the other and covering the miles in all weathers is a way of moving forward and, even if the future feels hopeless, it is a way of finding direction.

We talked for a while about the places she and her Labrador were headed and I shared my love of Northumberland, which luckily enough was one of her destinations. We talked about the coastal path, the castles and the rugged beauty of the landscape. I told her that the other benefit of walking with a dog is that people will stop and talk and that you can make those interactions as shallow or as deep as you want. I wished her well and I'll think about her when she's on her walk, knowing how much that dog will make her smile every day and how he will lead her onwards as best he can.

As for the other events at Goodwoof, they had a few sips of pun juice as they came up with ideas like 'Ministry of Hound', a music and dance session for dogs; 'Barkitecture', which is a kennel design competition; and 'Barkour', a dog version of parkour where people and their pets leap from one object to another. Think Tom Cruise in *Mission: Impossible*. In fact, the guy they've booked to showcase Barkour is Wade Eastwood – who really is the stunt coordinator for Tom Cruise.

They don't do things by half at Goodwood.

Every year, Goodwoof will focus on a different breed to kick off the festival and in 2023 it was poodles. No one was expecting the enthusiasm with which poodle owners leaped at the chance to gather outside Goodwood House at nine in the morning. They started arriving an hour early, and in the end, around 300 poodles of all sizes paraded from the house to the kennels. It was a comically grand way to start Goodwoof and with the blessing of sunshine and a cooling breeze, they celebrated a massively successful weekend.

Strolling around the grounds in black and orange uniforms with hats and orange gloves are the Gnawland Nannies (geddit?) who will take care of your dog for you if you need a break.

At the Puppy Petting area, I bump into some young girls who are desperate to take them home.

'I wish my mum would buy one. I *need* one,' one of them lamented.

I had a chat with her, and it emerged she did actually already have a dog but was desperate for another. She was pacified by a long petting session with a warm and willing puppy.

* * *

Claire Mannion was one of the leaders of the team that put on Goodwoof. She went to see the other dog festivals to learn what worked and what didn't, then created something that is different on every level. We have a walk around the site together to appreciate the different areas. Everything looked beautiful, as if it had been designed by an architect. Turns out, it was.

'We want to do things that you wouldn't expect, and to do it in our own way,' she tells me. 'The duke is very design led and he wants it to be authentic. He knows every detail and is involved in everything.'

I pause at the large Doga studio. Yes, that's yoga with dogs – or puppy yoga for all ages. About sixty people were on mats stretching out and breathing deeply. An instructor on the stage in the middle had a dog alongside her, as did everyone else. The aura of calm clearly suited them, as most of the dogs were taking the opportunity for a quick nap. There is no greater compliment a dog can pay a yoga instructor than falling asleep in their session.

There are also massages available, sound bathing (I'm not really sure how that works; it's something to do with music), reiki and even tarot card reading. Yes, I do mean tarot card reading for dogs. I think they may have moved on to the wine when they came up with that one.

There is a massive shallow pool called Fido's Lido with beach huts, agility that anyone can have a go at, sheepdog demonstrations and CaniCross. There are people who know what they're doing competing against each other and then 'have a go' demonstrations for people who want to try it for the first time.

If you haven't heard of CaniCross, it's cross-country running with a dog out in front of you, connected to you by a harness and lead. They also do it on bicycles and scooters, which looks a bit hairy to me. They were getting up to 28mph on the bikes at Goodwoof and if you're going that fast, you need to make sure you're in control of the dog who is leading you. The idea was originally a way of keeping huskies fit and active in the summer months when they couldn't drag sleds through the snow and it's been adapted as a sport for all people and all dogs.

I'd suggest some breeds are better suited than others. I wouldn't think a Chihuahua would enjoy it as much as say, a German shepherd, a pointer or a border collie, but I'm willing to be proved wrong. I met a woman recently who'd done it with her tiny little poodle-cross, who was barely a foot high, so it can be done.

The most important thing is that your dog understands commands to tell them to go, turn left ('haw') or right ('gee') and most of all, that they know when to *stop*. You don't want your dog leading you at full pace into a river, however much they might enjoy it.

The Duke of Richmond hosted a drinks party on the Saturday night of Goodwoof and invited everyone who had played a key role in its success: the designers who had entered kennels into the Barkitecture awards, the agility and flyball experts and the CaniCross competitors. I start chatting to them as we sip champagne in the evening sun under an ancient Lebanon cedar. It's a tough life …

The CaniCross gang are all good friends, bonded by the fun they have with their dogs, and I'm struck by the same thoughts I had about the agility world – dogs can create an amazing community of friends and they can embed us in groups that we would never have met any other way.

They explained to me that if they go to a running club, they will get lots of questions about themselves, whereas if you go to CaniCross, all the questions are about the dog. It takes the focus off you and even in the competition, the pressure is off because it's not just about your performance. Sometimes the dog goes wrong, or doesn't fancy it, or stops for a pee – and you can always blame that.

One of the women tells me that CaniCross is her one escape in life. She means it. She had been through a really tough time in her relationship and had got very low. She discovered CaniCross and she says it saved her. It helped her recover her confidence and her sense of identity, and gave her a reason to exercise, which started to make her feel healthier and better. She races every weekend and it provides her with a social life in a completely different environment from work or home.

Another woman watched the CaniCross demonstration at Crufts and told me that it dawned on her that she didn't need to be a Lycra-clad goddess to take part, that it was a sport for everyone. It gave her a break from elderly parents who were not well and the chance to let her mind clear. She soon got faster, fitter and fell in love with it. She runs and cycles behind her dogs and competes almost every weekend.

There is no prize money on offer, but the benefit for the participants is clearly far more valuable than money.

Cushla Lamen was one of the people who helped introduce CaniCross to the UK over 20 years ago. She was in Germany where her husband was posted in the army and got her first dog, a husky. She took up running to give the dog enough exercise and then heard about this new sport from a friend. The first CaniCross race in the UK was staged in the Forest of Dean in 2002. Cushla was there.

'I thought, this is my dream, this is what I want to do, and I've been passionate about it ever since,' she tells me.

She helps run the CaniCross Facebook group, which has many thousands of followers and a map with all the clubs in the UK and across Europe.

'You can borrow harnesses and leads from those clubs to give it a try and see if you and your dog like it before investing in buying the kit yourself,' she says. 'There are lots of club events and we've also got national championships and you qualify from those to get to the world championships, which are staged all over the place. The race categories are broken down into age and gender so at least we've all got a chance.'

Some top-level track athletes make the leap to Cani-Cross and find it a really fun environment that gives them the competitive life they enjoy, but you don't have to be able to do a 5k in under half an hour to take part.

Cushla says the best courses are between 5 and 6km and involve lots of turns to keep the dogs interested. She likes Thetford Forest because it's got a really good, well-drained surface for the dogs' feet and has lots of variety. She starts the training from the early years.

'We've got a couple of rehomed dogs and a couple we've had since puppies and we'll train them from very young to understand the commands, but you do get squirrel moments when you think everything is going really well and suddenly you find yourself halfway up a tree because your dog has decided to chase a squirrel.'

I can see that this is a good option for active dogs that sometimes get frustrated or bored with everyday walks. It's also a great way for their owners to challenge themselves and maintain a high fitness level.

'So many dogs which are aggressive on a lead are much happier when you put them in a harness and give them a job to do. ' Cushla says. 'Dogs just want jobs. It can be something so simple. You've got dogs with limited recall, dogs that don't want to be in tight spaces, but give them a role, put them in a situation that suits them and you've got a different dog.'

Cushla says she advises people to only use the CaniCross harness when they're training or in competition. If you want a dog just to go for a fun walk, use a normal lead. They will understand.

There are plans to extend the idea of 'BarkRun', the CaniCross equivalent of parkrun. There are also 'have a go' sessions at all the major dog festivals if you want to give it a go.

In her day job, Cushla gives clinical massages to dogs that need muscle therapy; she understands the injuries that dogs can acquire from chasing balls or running on rough surfaces, so she is always making sure that things are done correctly at CaniCross. She has a pointer crossed with a greyhound called Mayhem as her racing dog, and although she says he can be very naughty, he is clearly very good at it.

The CaniCross gang head off into the evening sunset and tell me they're going to get an early night because they're running again the next day. They are positively buzzing.

* * *

Goodwoof's chosen charity, which benefitted from the auction of the Barkitecture display, was Pets As Therapy.

PAT takes dogs and cats to visit people who might need the comfort of an animal but don't have access to one of their own. They have four and a half thousand volunteers across the UK and are using the festival as a way of talking to more potential supporters and raising awareness of what they do. It's a very simple concept and people who love dogs get a real kick out of sharing that love with someone who can't have their own pet.

Pets As Therapy look for dogs that are confident but not over-enthusiastic. In other words, not a dog like Boris the boxer. The very idea of him going into a care home or a hospice is horrifying. Imagine ten stone of boundless boxer energy coming towards your ailing grandmother at pace. It's not a comforting thought.

Many other dogs, however, are hugely suitable for the role, and do a brilliant job in hospitals, care homes and schools. Size is irrelevant. They can be as big as a St Bernard or as small as a Pomeranian; it doesn't matter as long as they like people and are happy to be petted by a stranger.

If you volunteer your dog for Pets As Therapy, they will give them a full body exam to make sure there are no sensitive areas that might cause an adverse reaction when someone is stroking them. They also do a sudden-noise test to see how they react and how quickly they recover.

The auction of the Barkitecture display raised more than £30,000 for Pets As Therapy.

'We put on events to make people smile and have an enjoyable time,' Claire Mannion says. 'Honestly, I walk around and feel so proud of it when everyone is looking so happy.'

I came home with a warm glow after Goodwoof and made Alice promise that next year, she has to come with me.

CHAPTER 12

Service

Dogs in the military, the police force, the fire service, guard dogs, sniffer dogs, search and rescue dogs, dogs that can detect explosive devices: everywhere you look you will find service dogs doing jobs that man and machine cannot.

There is an award for animals that deserve recognition for outstanding service in society called the PDSA (People's Dispensary for Sick Animals) Gold Medal. It's for 'civilian dogs' and since it was instituted in 2002 it has been awarded 30 times. Many police dogs have been recognised for outstanding bravery but often, the medal goes to pets.

For example, a cockapoo called Teddy alerted the family and saved the life of five-year-old Riley, who has Down's Syndrome. Riley had climbed into the tumble dryer and shut the door, which set off the drying cycle and trapped him in there. If Teddy hadn't frantically barked, Riley's parents would have had no idea that he was in trouble. Riley had burns to his arms, back and head, but it could have been so much worse were it not for Teddy's quick and insistent reaction.

The military version is the PDSA Dickin Medal, first awarded in 1943. Named after the founder of the PDSA, Maria Dickin, it is given to animals to recognise outstanding acts of bravery or devotion to duty in the armed forces or civil defence units across the world. It's the animal equivalent of the Victoria Cross. To date, 75 animals have been awarded the PDSA Dickin Medal: 38 dogs, 32 pigeons, 4 horses and 1 cat.

Six of the last nine winners have been Belgian Malinois. Originally bred as herding dogs in Belgium, they are smaller, sleeker versions of a German shepherd and are often employed as police and military dogs. They are alert, quick to respond, sensitive and very keen to work. Many Belgian Malinois served in Afghanistan detecting improvised explosive devices or flushing out and incapacitating enemy insurgents.

A PDSA Dickin Award to a different breed catches my eye because it's for detecting electronic devices like mobile phones, voice recorders or GPS devices.

Hertz (a German short-haired pointer) was the first dog trained by the Royal Air Force Police to detect personal electronic devices. It's a procedure often required by the prison service to find illegal mobile phones but had never before been used in a military situation. The citation for Hertz says he 'was at the cutting edge of defending troops from the ever-evolving advances in digital intelligence'.

These dogs have been highly trained and are working in exceptional circumstances, but you don't have to leave it to the forces. Your dog could learn to sniff out different items, just for the fun of it. Dogs can be trained to detect truffles, lost items of clothing or even mobile phones.

I am becoming ever more aware that stimulation is as important to dogs as exercise and food. Just like us, they get bored if they're not given enough to do. That's why they end up destroying the sofa or chewing your shoes.

Sandie's Scent School in Worcestershire takes the basics of police training to dogs in normal life to help them develop a natural talent. Similar to agility and CaniCross but suiting a different skill set, this is a way of keeping dogs active and interested. It also increases the bond between owner and dog because they are doing something with you and for you.

Sandie Dallow joined the police force in 1991 with dreams of becoming a dog handler. There were no women in that role in her branch and it took her five years to get the chance. She spent the next 25 years in the dog section working with all sorts of dogs who could sniff out firearms, drugs and cash.

Sandie loved her job and she loved the dogs she worked with. She had all sorts but it seems German shepherds or German shepherd-crosses were often the best.

Often, she would have to role-play to disguise the fact that her dog was searching for drugs. She would dress in civilian clothes, walk hand in hand with another officer and let her dog sniff around the area where they thought stolen goods might be hidden. On one such innocent-looking walk, her dog Bruno found £60,000 worth of cocaine buried under a tree. Bruno was also responsible for her most successful find.

Her colleagues assured her the garage had already been searched and was clear, but when she went in there, Bruno started to try to climb up the wall. She tried to work out why he wanted to get up to the top of the building so looked up into the rafters and saw the corner of a red bag. The bag contained a cricket ball-sized haul of cocaine and another bag full of a distinctive cutting agent. Based on that find, 12 people were sent to prison.

I suggest that dogs would be better judges of a guilty individual in a line-up than human beings. We are never quite sure of what we have seen, nor do we remember features accurately, but dogs never forget a scent. Sadly, their identification cannot be used in a court of law. More fool us.

As Sandie neared retirement age, she wanted to find a way to continue working with dogs and using all the skills she had learned to help people get the best out of their dogs. She had seen how much her dogs enjoyed using their superior sense of smell in challenging situations and how much they wanted to please their owners, so she started Sandie's Scent School to help train ordinary dogs to identify certain scents and find hidden items.

To see her training and her pupils in action, Alice and I have driven to Worcestershire County Cricket Club on the banks of the River Severn. We both like cricket and would happily take in a game, but we're not here to admire the batsmen practising hitting sixes. I am slightly worried that my car, parked outside the stand to which they are hitting, may be in danger of getting its windscreen smashed. I'll be very impressed with the batsman, obviously, but it will make the drive home a little difficult.

If you have a picture in your head of a retired police dog handler, that image will no doubt resemble Sandie. She seems young to be retired, but that's the way it is with the police force. She is fit and strong, no-nonsense in her approach and uses phrases like 'we will apprehend the suspects'.

Sandie has four Scent School attendees today. Alan the wirehaired vizsla, Mabel the Rhodesian ridgeback, Archie the Labrador and Jet the cocker spaniel. They are all on the 'Constable Course', and their initial scent is gun oil.

Not many people have gun oil hanging around at home, but Sandie is not like most people. Not only does she have gun oil, she also has small magnetic sliding tins in which to put a drop of it on a piece of cotton wool. I stick my nose in to have a whiff and it's strong, but not overwhelming.

The dogs already know the scent, and Sandie hides the tin in between some seats in one of the stands of the cricket ground. Being an ex-police officer, she doesn't just play a game of hide and seek. Instead, she sets up a 'crime scene'. The scenario today is that four women on a hen party have streaked across the cricket ground, disturbing the match. Three have been apprehended but one has escaped. They have left behind various clues in the form of jewellery and shoes.

If you're thinking actual diamonds or high-heeled shoes, think a bit smaller. You know those tiny accessories you get with dolls? That's what Sandie is using, and that's the evidence each owner must retrieve to prove they have found the scent.

Alan and his owner Stacey are set on the trail. Alan takes his time but when he stops at the seat where the tin is hidden, Stacey rewards him. She finds the tiny plastic tiara and proudly takes it to show Sandie.

Stacey has told me that Alan was a lockdown puppy who couldn't get the socialisation he needed. He didn't know how to play and was very nervous around other dogs and people. He's just over two years old now and is a transformed character.

'Doing this has really helped his confidence. It's brought him out of his shell,' Stacey says.

Jet the black cocker spaniel has an advantage, because he was trained to be a sniffer dog but he didn't make the grade. He took early retirement at 14 months old and was moved on to be a pet. Now that he's a bit older, his owner Charlie has worked out that even if he didn't make it as a full-time sniffer dog, he really wants to use his nose.

'He loves it now, so I think he just needed to grow into it. It's so much mental enrichment for him,' she tells me.

'On a rainy day, it's a good way of tiring him out if we can't go out for a long walk because I can hide things around the house and he loves to find them. It fulfils their natural foraging instinct as well.'

Jet is very fast, his tail wagging all the time as he moves along the rows of seats, barely pausing until he finds the scent of gun oil. He stops and points his nose to where the tin is hidden. Charlie rewards him and he looks very pleased with himself.

Sandie explains the benefits of the training that are about more than sniffing out lost items.

'It makes you work as a team,' she says. 'It makes you understand your dog and communicate much better with them. It can also build up their confidence and give them a sense of purpose. I've got so many examples of dogs who have issues that have been transformed by scent work.'

Alice asks if certain breeds are better at it than others, but Sandie is happy to work with any dog, from French bull-dogs to bloodhounds. She says it's about finding the right incentive so that the dog is doing it for a reason.

Sandie runs various levels of courses, so a dog can grad-uate from Constable to Sergeant to Inspector. Constable level is one scent, a second scent (cloves) is added for Sergeant and then a third scent for the promotion to Inspector.

Alice and I have watched a lot of *Line of Duty* and are worried about the potential for corruption within the police dog section. Our fears are misplaced. These are honest dogs who only want to please. I point out that if dogs can be trained to sniff out cash, she could turn this into a very, very profitable course.

Sandie smiles at me in what I hope is not a disapproving manner.

I ask her how much is it about training dogs and how much is it training people? She doesn't hesitate.

'It's training people. Dogs are easy but people can be, you know …'

'Muppets?' I suggest.

'Well, I wouldn't say that, but they're sometimes unaware of what their dogs can do and how to get the best out of them.'

Sandie tells me the story of a man who got a black Russian terrier from Poland. He bought it on the internet. I have seen black Russian terriers at Crufts. They are huge and they need really disciplined training and plenty of stimulation. He had failed to understand the responsibility and had no relationship with the dog at all.

He took it to Crufts but it got disqualified for biting the judge. Yup, that'll get you kicked out. The poor dog had a very tender spot on its leg and when the judge went to examine it, the dog felt pain and lashed out. The owner had not bothered to put it on anti-inflammatory drugs or treat the sore in any way because, he said, 'What's the point? Once they've worn off, you've still got the problem. It's a big dog, it's going to cost me a lot of money.'

He ended up having to have the dog put down.

Stories like this make me so angry, because it's basic ignorance combined with a lack of compassion.

Sandie says she is often tempted to tell people that they should leave their dog with her because they're not capable of having one. I think she should be put in charge of any new guidelines for responsible dog ownership. She knows what she's on about and she understands the best and worst of human nature as much as she understands dog.

* * *

As Alice and I head back home, I tell her that Sandie runs murder mystery weekends for people with their dogs. I say that it might be fun to try one.

'Don't even think about it,' she says.

You see, this is why we work as a couple. We are not the same.

Alice is much cleverer than me for starters, and she's funnier. I make up for what I lack in intelligence by overwhelming enthusiasm, whereas she is more cautious, wanting to know the reasons for doing something before we turn up. She would be a very good guard dog. I would be useless because I'd wag my tail and try to make friends with the intruder.

Now that we film *Celebrity Gogglebox* together, Alice is having to adapt to being recognised. For decades she has enjoyed the anonymity of radio with only die-hard Radio 4 fans asking her to do the Shipping Forecast as her party trick. Now, she has complete strangers telling her they love her on *Gogglebox*. They are right to love her. When I was asked to do the celebrity version, I wasn't sure. I love the series and I didn't want to ruin the fun of watching it by being in it. I was also worried about the intrusion and the time it would take but then they suggested that Alice and I did it together.

We thought about the benefits – we could do it from home, it's not that onerous (contrary to popular opinion, you don't have a camera crew in your sitting room every evening) and best of all, you get a hamper full of goodies. We even get to choose our own treats so I can have sweet-and-salty popcorn and Alice can have Galaxy chocolate.

On a more serious note, we are conscious that we can be helpful to other same-sex couples who struggle for acceptance within their own families. There are loads of ways of changing attitudes, to help the world not just accept or tolerate our relationship but actively embrace and respect it. This seemed like one of them. People talk about 'normalising' behaviour and there couldn't be anything more normal than a couple who've been together for over 20 years sitting together on the sofa at home, watching TV.

We may bicker in the car but we rarely, if ever, argue. We have the same moral compass and I will discuss every work decision with Alice before I accept or reject it. She makes sure I take good breaks from work but will also send me off to the study to do my prep for the Coronation or for Wimbledon, or to do some writing. Sometimes I think she does it to get me out of the room. She defends me if I am being attacked and keeps me grounded if I am flying high. We celebrate together and we grieve together but most of all we have fun together, and there's no one I would rather be with on holiday or at home.

Getting another dog is not just about finding the right one for us, it's about us being in the right place and space for the dog, and I understand now that I left too much of the responsibility for Archie to Alice. Next time, I need to be more present and I need to be consistent with my voice and my behaviour so that our dog knows that they don't have to be in charge.

The last year of exploring the British Isles to research this book, meeting dog breeders, owners and all sorts of dog lovers, has meant that I've thought a lot about what we do next. What breed of dog do we want, where will it come from and when will we be ready for it to come into our family?

I recently went to visit the Dogs Trust centre near my family home. It is in a converted farm in Hamstead Marshall, just outside Newbury, with 36 kennels that have recently been refurbished so they all look super-smart and comfortable for the dogs, with underfloor heating and lots of light. They have outdoor play areas, a training barn, a puppy suite and a vet suite.

The Canine Defence League was established in 1891 during the first Cruft's show. In 2003 it changed its name to the Dogs Trust and is the largest dog welfare charity in the UK with 22 rehoming centres across the UK and Ireland. Here's the starkest and most frightening fact – never in its history has it known a higher number of handover requests than it's getting right now.

In 2019, the number of dogs needing to be rehomed through the Dogs Trust was 23,000. In 2022 it was more than 50,000. It doesn't take a maths genius to work out that is more than double, which really doesn't reflect well on us, the general public, or our understanding of what it takes to care for a dog properly.

Even across 21 homing centres in the UK and one in Ireland, the Dogs Trust doesn't have room to meet escalating demand. Pre-Covid, they had about 50 handover requests a day. Now, they receive more than 125 every single day.

As I'm shown around, I ask the assistant manager of operations Rhian Grey and the assistant manager of administration Natasha Tarrant about the reasons for rehoming. The financial strain being felt across the country has meant that a lot of dogs come in because they need urgent expensive veterinary care which is beyond the scope of their owners.

Tash tells me that as a way of trying to help keep dogs in their homes, the Dogs Trust has set up a new temporary relief fund which can help with a one-off cost of an operation. It's early days with the fund but it should help alleviate the problem. They are also expanding their use of foster carers so that dogs can live in someone's house, rather than kennels, before it finds a long-term home.

Other dogs have behavioural problems like guarding issues (just as Archie did with a pair of socks), aggression towards strangers or other dogs, separation anxiety because of lack of socialisation during lockdown or they are former street dogs who haven't been able to adapt to domestic life. The overwhelming reason for dogs arriving here is that the owners just can't cope any more.

In spacious individual kennels behind glass doors, with plenty of soft cushions, beds and toys, I meet River, a one-year-old Saluki-cross who looks like an elegant lurcher. Her bio explains that she is very playful and energetic but she doesn't like to be left for a long time on her own. She can live with another dog but she cannot cope with cats, so that rules her out for us but later, I mention River to my mother in the hope she might go and have a look at her.

There are certain breeds that seem to be over-represented at the Dogs Trust, which in itself tells a story. They have a lot of bulldog and Staffie-crosses, cockapoos and collie-crosses and, the one that I find most surprising, dachshunds.

The explanation is to do with puppy smuggling. The demand for dachshunds (particularly after Maisie the wire-haired dachshund won Crufts in 2020) meant that there was a lot of activity in the puppy smuggling market, with either puppies or pregnant bitches being brought into the country by criminal gangs.

More than two thousand puppies have been seized by the Border Force since 2015 and taken into Dogs Trust care. Since 2021, there has been a 60 per cent increase in the number of pregnant bitches seized, many of them being smuggled in to satisfy the Christmas market. The numbers swell over November and December. You can see now why the charity adopted the slogan 'a dog is for life, not just for Christmas' and adapted during Covid to: 'a dog is for life, not just for lockdown'.

Our propensity to buy things on demand with the click of a button means that adults have been shopping online for puppies as if they were toys, with no understanding of how that is fuelling the illegal puppy smuggling market. There is also a misconception that buying at a higher price ensures quality. It doesn't. The smugglers may charge more than legitimate, responsible breeders.

For all that we know about the joy dogs can bring to our lives, and of course this book is a celebration of that relationship, the stories I hear about each dog at the Dogs Trust paint a painful picture. This is what happens when humans do not understand the responsibility of bringing a dog into the family and how lack of research and care has created an overblown market for 'greeders', smugglers and puppy farms.

The rehoming process at the Dogs Trust is a long and patient one which involves studying the dog's history (if indeed it is accurate) and observing its behaviour. When it works, it's the most rewarding benefit for the team who work there.

'We had a dog here called Bertie, who had been here pretty much his whole life,' Rhian tells me. 'The first rehome didn't work out, but we recently found him a family who are willing to take him on and work with his anxiety, and that's so rewarding because he's so happy. The most upsetting thing is when a dog comes in a terrible condition or when the owner hasn't noticed a head tilt, for example, that might be a sign of serious pain.'

In some instances, the dog may have been behaving badly or snapping when it's touched, but that's because it was hurting and the owner didn't realise it needed to go to the vet.

Outside on an area of lawn with a wooden bench, I meet Percy, who has only arrived three days ago from Penrith in Cumbria. He is a friendly little chap with a blonde long-haired coat which feels quite soft to the touch. He looks very well and healthy, and happily sits on my lap to take a treat. The team tell me that he's been friendly with other dogs and is good on the lead. I would say he was a cross between a dachshund and a Yorkshire terrier, with maybe a bit of Jack Russell or even Dandie Dinmont.

Percy was found as a stray in Ireland, which means there is very little background information so even his age is a bit of a mystery, but they have estimated he is between five and seven years old. Spending ten minutes with Percy, I can tell he won't be here long and Tash tells me that after posting his profile, the centre was overrun with enquiries. It's now down to the team to do the background checks and make sure that whoever takes him will be able to give him a loving and caring home for the rest of his life.

Yes, of course I was tempted to take him home with me, and I have been in touch since to check on his progress. I have also developed a habit of scanning the Dogs Trust pages to keep an eye on what's going on.

*　*　*

As my journey across our isle of dogs draws to an close, I reflect on what I have discovered. I thought I knew a lot about dogs, but the joy of this animal is that there is always so much more to learn. I see so many wonderful breeders and dog owners at Crufts every year, I meet them every day as I walk through parks or visit dog festivals and I know that here in the UK we have been at the forefront of training dogs to do all sorts of jobs, from detection to assistance. I think we do have a special relationship with dogs, a respect for them and a genuine love for the way in which they enhance our world. There is, for example, a growing use of dogs in our schools to help reluctant readers or children who have anxiety and I love that as a solution. Dogs can help heal us; they enhance our social skills and both our physical and mental health. However, we have a huge responsibility and we need to ensure that our knowledge as owners, custodians of these brilliant creatures, continues to grow too. Right now, there are too many dogs being acquired from dubious sources, who are poorly trained or have been poorly socialised in lockdown conditions, and whose welfare is not properly understood by their owners. It's vital that, to maintain the bond between us and our dogs, we educate ourselves and help the authorities clamp down on illegal puppy farms, on puppy smuggling, and that the Kennel

Club uses its influence to continue campaigning for tighter licensing of breeders.

When it comes to Alice and me, we've probably learned more from *not* having a dog than from having one, thanks to the research we've done for this book. I thought that decent food and two walks a day was the key, but I now understand how lucky we were to have Archie for as long as we did. He could have got a lot worse in his guarding behaviour and it was only by warning visitors to be careful that we got away with him not causing serious injury.

Next time, we need to do better, and that means not moving into a new house while work is still ongoing, making sure we are consistent with our training, that we provide early socialisation and plenty of stimulation, as well as exercise, and that we remain calmly and kindly at the top of the pecking order.

There is no quick and easy fix, but maybe that's a better message all round. We shouldn't be able to click a button and have a dog arrive by post to fill a hole in our lives. We should have to think about it, work at it and be properly prepared. That's why the rescue charities ask so many questions and why they make it so difficult for people to adopt, and it's also why the Dogs Trust or Battersea will be our first port of call when we have the right set-up to offer a dog the perfect home. I've met many breeds in my life, and I've got to know some of them a lot better in this last year, and so on that question I am keeping an open mind: while different breeds offer different delights, it's also a case of finding the dog whose temperament best suits our situation, and whose needs we can best honour. I've discovered the many ways that dogs offer us their service – but more important is to offer them ours.

My big hope is that my mother will get another dog sooner rather than later, so that I can offer to help with the training. It would transform her life to have a dog that comes back when it's called, is small enough to be scooped up into the back of the car and offers her friendship and good company. She might even let me borrow it now and again. You never know.

Just as I'm finishing this book, the Dogs Trust write to me with some good news:

> Just to let you know Percy is now reserved and is having his first meet this morning. Which is great. Keeping everything crossed for a successful meet.

I'm delighted to hear it. After all, every dog must have his day.

Epilogue

When we shot the cover photo for this book I wanted a range of breeds that would cover some of the key dogs I'd written about. So we have Susie the boxer, Narla the lurcher, Marco the Jack Russell terrier and DX the Labrador. They all have an agent as well.

Sandra Strong runs the agency Dogs on Camera, and she is the lead trainer at Perfect Dog, which prepares dogs for the world of stage and screen.

She started her working life in theatre and studied theatre design at Wimbledon School of Arts, then became a veterinary nurse and finally combined her interests to work with dogs in show business. She founded Dogs on Camera in 2002 and has more than a hundred dogs on her books. Marco is her own dog and is sitting on her lap as we chat during the lunch break.

I ask her about the key to success – for the dogs, obviously.

'They have to have good habituation and early socialisation. You have to get the training in as soon as possible. This is a lovely quiet studio,' she says – to my relief. 'But often it's noisy and distracting and they have to be bomb-proof.'

All of the dogs are very relaxed for our cover shoot. I've dragged a rug from my make-up room so that the dogs can lie on it. Narla has happily taken that option, whereas Susie and DX prefer the sofa and Marco is sitting between Sandra's legs. I ask her about the sort of things she has to train her dogs to do.

'My first film was a remake of *St Trinian's* and I remember them ringing me up and saying, "you're the last resort". Quite a lot of people used to say that, and I was thinking of calling the agency The Last Resort, but then decided it didn't send the right message. Anyway, they told me they needed a dog to shag someone's leg.'

She pauses and I don't know what to say. I wasn't expecting that. I had foolishly been thinking of dogs in action roles or as detectives or a key component of an epic love story. It hadn't occurred to me that an agent would be providing dogs who can hump a leg on demand.

Sandra continues.

'Oh, I said, that's not a problem, I've got one of those, but it comes with its leg.'

I assumed she meant a rubber or a plastic leg but no, she means an actual leg.

'It only wanted to shag the leg of its dog walker, you see.'

Right. My mind is working fast and I can see a leg double working pretty well.

Epilogue

'They asked what kind of dog it was and I told them it was a cavalier King Charles spaniel and they said they didn't want one of those, they wanted a terrier.'

Jeez, the fickle nature of the film world. You've got a perfectly good candidate who can actually do the stunt they want, but no, that's not the look they're going for. I would have slammed down the phone, but this is why Sandra has been a success in this industry and I would not be. She looked immediately for a solution.

'OK, I thought. Well, I've got my own terriers. This was before him of course.' She points down at Marco, who is looking as if butter wouldn't melt in his mouth. 'None of the boys wanted to do it, so I thought I'd try the girls. I knew from my days as a veterinary nurse how to get dogs to feel a bit randy, so I thought I'd try the experiment on Dolly and she went crazy for it.'

Now, forgive my lack of journalistic instinct, but I didn't ask what it was that Sandra did to trigger Dolly's libido. I think I was still in shock.

'Fifteen minutes, she was giving it her all on my leg,' Sandra says with obvious pride. 'And she got the part! I asked them if they wanted to see what else she could do but the only thing they were interested in was the humping. Her cue for it was "go for it, Dolls!" and it worked every time.'

Sandra had effectively created a canine porn star and her work got noticed. She was contacted to provide a dog for a scene in *The Inbetweeners* that I don't want to even describe in the pages of what is meant to be a family book. Suffice to say it's not behaviour you want your dog to replicate.

This niche sideline of depravity apart, Sandra has placed dogs in rather more genteel and respectable roles. She provided a lot of dogs for *Britain's Favourite Dog* on ITV and for a series of Land Rover adverts.

The rules surrounding dog performance are strict. Sandra explains: 'All dogs have to be licensed and insured. You can't just grab the producer's dog because you like the look of it. I generally like a vet on board as well and they will often give the health and safety briefing, but it's always good to have back-up in case you're asked to do something that you think is not safe, like send your dog into a fast-running stream or ask it to jump off a height that is too far.'

On every shoot, Sandra has the dog's best interests at heart. She won't let them do things that are dangerous and she will call a stop to filming if the dog is not happy. She is an expert in calming signals. There are more than 130 signals that a dog gives off to show distress and she will keep an eye on them to see whether there are any early warning signals. She tells me that an adult dog can work for six hours but there are always breaks so it works out as between twenty and forty minutes in each hour. And as for money, I'm sure you're interested in what she charges for each dog.

It varies greatly depending on the requirements of the project, but when she tells me the highest fees could be in excess of £1,000 a day, I whistle. She looks at me sternly and explains that it's more than worth it.

'Think about the preparation for a dog that needs a lot of grooming like an Afghan hound or a poodle, and they need a handler, so there's a lot going on with each dog.'

Apart from the grooming of dogs with extravagant hairstyles, the training for specific tricks is the biggest challenge. Sandra says it's fine if they stick to what they've asked for but of course we TV types are so damned fickle. Things are always changing and even if the producer or the director insists they've made it simpler, it won't be if the trick you've trained the dog to do has changed.

'I had one request for an advert which was originally for a dog to run down the corridor towards the camera, which was easy enough,' Sandra says. 'Then they said they wanted it to run into a room, pick up a parcel from under a tree, rip it open, take out a jumper that's inside the parcel and run round the room with it and then run out of the room. I barely had two days with the dog to train it to do this and what I didn't know was that the dog was terrified of jumpers because it had once chewed up its owner's jumper and got told off for it. So I asked if it could be a teddy bear rather than a jumper.

'Then when we went to the shoot, all they wanted it to do was carry the parcel down the hallway – but of course once you've taught a dog that it can rip a parcel to bits, that's way more fun to do! So that was a challenge. We did it, but honestly, it was tough.'

Having worked in the theatre with human actors and now with canine performers, I ask Sandra which is easier to deal with. She doesn't hesitate.

'Dogs. Every time.'

We resume our photo shoot with Marco next to me behind a table. In return for a treat (every performer needs payment), he puts his paws onto the surface and stares towards Sandra. I look the same way and Alex captures the shot you see on the cover.

However you define 'star quality', I'd say Marco has got it.

Afterword:

Alice has the last word …

When Archie had to be put down over lockdown, it broke our hearts. I wanted so much for him to die in his sleep. I couldn't even call the vet to make the appointment so Clare had to do it.

We knew the vet had to be Vesi. As Clare has said, Archie loved the vet. I don't mean he tolerated it, no, he positively looked forward to his visits. His tail wagged when he stood outside the door. He would rush in and stand himself on the weighing machine, looking at the receptionist as if to say, 'Look what a good boy I am! Can I have a treat now?' When we were in the waiting room and the vet would come out to announce the name of the next patient, Archie would rush to go in, even if it wasn't his turn.

When Archie was about ten years old, he developed a nasty ulcer and had to have the end of his tail amputated. Removing any bit of the tail is a very painful process (don't get me started on docking) and after the operation, Archie had to have a bandage on the end of his tail. Twice-weekly visits to Vesi ensured that it was healing properly, and then the time came for the bandage to be removed.

The tail was perfect; Archie was not. He was very upset and constantly looked at his tail. Back to Vesi we went. She suggested that maybe he was imagining pain from the part of the tail that was no longer there. She bandaged up the perfectly good tail and Archie was happy. I wondered if he was secretly finding ways to go and see Vesi. The bandage had to stay on for weeks longer than necessary, just to placate him.

So it was that Vesi had to do the final deed. Clare rang the vet on the Thursday, but Vesi wasn't able to see Archie until the Monday. It was the longest weekend of our lives. Counting out the meals that Archie had left. Looking at him and knowing that a few days later he wouldn't be there. We carried him up the stairs to bed with us every night and then down again two or three times so that he could go out into the garden, as his bladder was weak.

There is no doubt that it was time, but it was so painful.

The only thing that kept us sane was Button producing her five perfect kittens just three weeks earlier. Lockdown meant that it was easier to breed her than to have her spayed, as vets were only doing critical operations. We picked her 'husband', Max, and dropped her off in a cage outside his door. We were not allowed in because of lockdown, so we left her with Max and he did what tomcats are meant to do. I hope he was gentle with her.

We were sent a video of the two of them, but I thought it was more polite to avert our eyes. Two months later, Button meowed at me in a way I hadn't heard before. She was in labour. I took her up to the study where we had carefully prepared her birthing box. She was not interested in the birthing box. She had her kittens all over the floor in the study and we watched in awe and wonder.

She tried to have the first one in her litter tray. I had read that this would be disastrous as the litter would stick to the kitten and the mother would be unable to get the kitten dry and warm. I lifted her gently out of the tray and saw two tiny back legs sticking out of her rear end. I knew this was all sorts of wrong. Her first kitten was breech. So I pulled it out. It was alive and well. By kitten number three, Button had completely got the hang of it. She was a brilliant mother and the kittens were stunning.

It took six hours for all the kittens to be born, on the hottest day of the year. After about four hours we got a text from our lovely neighbours, who were part of the WhatsApp group Clare had set up. It simply said, 'Your supper is on the doorstep.' Thank you, Rosie and Giles – we have never forgotten that act of kindness.

Each morning we would wake up and go in to see them. They would crawl all over us and we watched them grow daily, weighing them on a tiny set of scales to check they were all making progress. They had gorgeous furry tummies and if anyone can resist snuggling their face into a kitten's tummy then, frankly, they are no friend of mine.

So it was that we had six cats and no dog. Four of the kittens went to friends and family and we kept Eric, because he was shy and actually the most beautiful. Also, we wanted a boy in the family. He continues to be shy, but in the mornings he comes up onto the sofa with me and rolls on his back so that I can rub his tummy ... for hours. He is ostensibly Clare's cat and Button is mine. Unlike his owner, Eric is not clever or outgoing.

We knew that we would have a substantial gap between losing Archie and getting another dog. Ideally, we would have a bigger garden and more space, so that involves moving house at some stage. This does not stop us thinking about it though. Our friend Dariel lost the gorgeous Sunny during lockdown. She got a Cavachon puppy called Pip.

Shortly after Pip's arrival, Dariel broke her shoulder and couldn't walk him, so we did. He was full of energy and bounced along to the park. We made it clear that if at any stage she didn't think she could cope with Pip, we would take him. It's very good news for Dariel (if not for us) that Pip has settled down and become the most perfect little chap. He is hugely pleased to see us when we visit and I like to think that he remembers us. In truth, I think he just loves everyone.

The project of finding another dog was Clare's motivation to write this book. I know that when we do find one I will take care of buying the dog food, making the visits to the vet and doing most of the grooming. Clare will be the one to provide long walks and, most of all, fun. Clare turns very puppy-like when she sees a dog. She's quite puppy-like anyway. Most people would say she resembles a bouncy Labrador and that is fairly accurate. She will talk to every dog she sees, ask the owner about its breeding, usually correctly identifying it even if it's an unusual crossbreed, and she'll make friends with complete strangers within seconds.

I have to drag her away and remind her that not everyone wants to talk.

Having read this book, I realise that I come across as rather curmudgeonly. It is not an inaccurate portrayal. As I have aged, I have become more and more grumpy. I have a very limited number of people I will tolerate for more than a couple of hours. I also get a migraine just by looking at a glass of wine, so I can't escape company by getting tiddly. This makes parties quite tedious. Clare, on the other hand, loves a party. There is nothing she likes more than getting her old friends together and throwing a good bash. I have been known to change into my pyjamas in order to encourage people to go home at two in the morning.

I have a couple of jobs in life, but there is one that surmounts all others and that is to try to make Clare happy. That means she has to have a dog in her life and I'm fine with that. It was one of the original commitments I made to her and I will never go back on it.

When we do find the right dog, we will endeavour to train it well. Let's face it, Clare has written enough about dog behaviour! However, my suspicion is that we will fail miserably.

After we conquer recall and possibly the 'sit' command, I know that the dog will be allowed to do absolutely anything he or she wants to. Our discipline will be hopeless. Our dog will be loved though. It will be loved in spades.

In our downstairs cloakroom, we have a carefully curated selection of photographs. Many of the photos are of our families. There is a whole wall dedicated to my father's war effort, of which I am immensely proud. He was awarded a Distinguished Service Cross and later, a *Légion d'honneur*, for his role in the Second World War raid on the port at St Nazaire, known as Operation Chariot.

Two photos, however, really stand out. One is of me petting a tame zebra in a lodge in Kenya, and one is of Clare feeding a baby panda in China. We have very, very blessed lives and wherever we go in the world we will try and connect with animals.

Clare may be more of a dog person and I am more of a cat person, but ultimately we both love all animals.

There are many people who watch Clare on the TV and think they know her. To be honest, they do, because she's just like that in real life. There are a couple of very funny sketches by the comedian and impressionist Tracey Ullman which depict Clare trying to help out with every single job, even if she doesn't know how to do it. They have to be informed by someone who knows her well. Even the depiction of 'Producer Sue' trying to rein her in is true. Our great friend Sue Butler used to be Clare's producer for various features on racing and other sports. She was constantly trying (unsuccessfully) to slow her down.

Clare likes to give unsolicited advice to all and sundry and her confidence is something to behold. On holiday recently we were given a padel tennis lesson. The rather dishy instructor asked if we spoke Italian.

'Not really,' replied Clare.

'Not really!' I exclaimed. 'We do *not* speak Italian. Any Italian. We know "prego", "pizza" and "spaghetti". This doesn't qualify as "not really".'

I guess this is a demonstration of Clare's willingness to please. She didn't want to offend them by saying no. She is a proper tail-wagger.

Clare has dragged me along on many of her research visits for this book. Don't tell her, but it hasn't been much of a hardship for me. I mean, it's not that awful having to cuddle a Labrador puppy that has fallen asleep during its training session. I can't claim that having a seven-week-old cocker spaniel puppy on my lap was too bad. I didn't even get the sneezes.

Short-haired dogs can be a problem, but I am more allergic to horses than dogs. Clare's father hugged me once when he had been out riding and I instantly came out in a rash. I had to persuade him that I wasn't allergic to him, it was the horsehair.

When Clare does a big sporting event, I am often asked if I am going too. There seems to be an assumption that as her partner, I would get tickets for the London Olympics or

Wimbledon, for example. The truth is, not only do I not get tickets but also, I generally don't go to work with Clare. Would you go to work with your partner if they were a doctor or an insurance broker?

Lovely as some of those events would be to attend as a fan, I have my own work to do, and if Clare is working then she is *working* – she doesn't need me hanging around making a nuisance of myself.

This book was a bit different. Clare wanted me to come and share in the doggie experience because ultimately, we are both invested in this. Also (as she has mentioned), she did all the driving. Again, don't tell her I said this, but she is actually a pretty good driver and we get there faster if I am in the passenger seat answering her emails and texts for her.

Also, I get to choose the music and I am a musical-theatre buff. My first job was in *Evita* and I've been hooked ever since. My role now with Mellow Magic Radio means that I get to present the Olivier Awards with the wonderful Ruthie Henshall, so I have to see as many of the shortlisted shows as possible. That is no hardship. It also means I can continue educating Clare about the world of musical theatre. It's a long haul. She once saw the musical *Mame* written down and pronounced it 'mah-may'. I mean, come on. Who doesn't know *Mame*?

I guess she knows obscure facts about sport that I don't; we all have our strengths.

Like many of the dogs in this book, Clare requires constant stimulation. When this is finished, she will move on to her next project with similar enthusiasm. People ask if I ever get to see her. Yes, all the time actually, and if she is away for more than a couple of nights, I really hate it. I never understand it if people think she is doing too much, because she doesn't have a regular show. Some presenters are on air every single day. She does lots of different things and the season tends to dictate that she's busy in the summer but not in the winter.

Her work ethic is what makes her so good at what she does, and she hates being unoccupied. Case in point: I left her one evening for a golf club board meeting. When I came home, she was nowhere to be seen. She had lasted exactly seven minutes on her own before popping over to Giles and Rosie's house down the road for a glass of rosé.

She doesn't do well on her own with nothing to do. Please bear this in mind if you are thinking of getting a collie or a working cocker. They will require the same sort of stimulation, but they need you to provide it. At least I know Clare can let herself out of the door and get on with whatever she needs to do.

Much as I come across as a glass-half-empty person, I prefer to see myself as the practical one (and it's just as well that one of us is). I can be boringly sensible; I know that. Clare is glass half full, waiting for a top-up. That top-up will eventually be a dog.

I will be allowed to name it and I am telling you now that I want to call it Nigel, even if it is a bitch.

I am in charge of finding the house and secure garden for us to bring up this dog. I look online almost every day for the perfect plot of land where we can build our dream home. The garden needs to be safe and secure and big enough for our dog to have a really good run around. We need to be near footpaths and maybe a dog-friendly park so that we can socialise with other dogs and dog owners.

Maybe not this year or next, but it's not too far in the future. Clare will no longer have to go on long walks without a lead in her hand. She will be happy and I will have, once again, fulfilled my promise to her.

Acknowledgements

It's a wonderful thing in life when you find a connecting force that will allow people to open up and speak freely. Dogs provide that magical key to friendship and shared experience, so I'd like to thank the dogs that have enriched my life so fully and brought so many people to the party. I suppose I should also thank my parents for introducing me to a life that revolved around dogs and for making me understand that dogs come higher up the pecking order than any child.

Huge thanks to Jessica Holm for her wonderful illustrations and for her wisdom and guidance. She has been a great source of information and a supportive voice telling me to keep doing it my way. Tom Reynolds has put up with me for years asking for random facts on the Olympics, Commonwealth Games and cycling, and now he has excelled himself in turning his hand to stories about dogs. Many thanks for his patience, his diligence and for reading an early draft with an expert sub-editor's eye for incorrect capitalisation of words and random use of numerals.

Ciara Farrell and Heidi Hudson at the Kennel Club have been wonderfully enthusiastic about this project and helped me with a generosity that you only find in people who love their subject so much that they want to share it with the widest possible audience. Thanks to Bob as well for sitting beside me and leaning in encouragingly as I made notes. He is a very supportive dog.

Then there are the people who let me spend time with them, observing what they do and asking endless questions: the teams at Battersea, the Dogs Trust and Dogs for Good are all doing amazing work with dogs and for dogs. I thank them for allowing me to intrude for a day.

Gill Raddings and her stunt dogs welcomed me into her home, as did Pat Whitehead, who also let me and Alice cuddle cocker spaniel puppies. Steve Jenkinson on Orkney imparted some fabulous information, as did Claire Guest at Medical Detection Dogs, Sandie Dallow at Sandie's Scent School and the fairy dogmother, Ellie Hart. Thanks to Toni Ilsley for her openness and honesty at Charlie's Place, to Charlotte Baker and Cushla Lamen for their enthusiasm for agility and Cani-Cross and for making me realise how much it had changed their lives.

Thanks to the Duke of Richmond, Claire Mannion and the whole team at Goodwoof for a fabulous weekend of fun. I will be back next year with Alice in tow.

I am hugely grateful to Fi Glover for sharing the joy of Nancy (and to Hector for a delicious roast chicken), Jennifer Saunders for doing the same with Olive and Andrew Cotter, along with his Olive and Mabel.

Acknowledgements

My editor, Robyn Drury, and my literary agent, Eugenie Furniss, have cajoled and encouraged me to get this all on paper, so thank you to them. Also to Joel Rickett, who first worked with me when he edited *My Animals and Other Family*. He is now a very big cheese in the publishing world and he gave the go-ahead for Ebury to publish *Isle of Dogs*, so I hope for his sake we can make this a bestseller!

I would like to thank Karen Gregor (and the gorgeous Oscar) for helping me set up all sorts of interviews and for being thoroughly invested in the project.

Most of all, thanks to Alice for letting me drag her along to all sorts of dog-related days out and for succumbing to my pleas to write her own chapter. She has also agreed to a complete lifestyle change, including moving house, so that we can create the perfect environment to welcome a dog into our lives once again. Watch this space.

Index

Index

Index

Index